TOP SECRET!

THE
POCKET GUIDE
TO

STUFF

TOP SECRET!

THE POCKET GUIDE TO

Boy

STUFF

BART KING

Illustrations by Chris Sabatino

GIBBS SMITH

TO ENRICH AND INSPIRE HUMANKIND

Salt Lake City | Charleston | Santa Fe | Santa Barbara

First Edition
13 12 11 10 09   10 9 8 7 6 5 4 3 2 1

Published by
Gibbs Smith
P.O. Box 667
Layton, Utah 84041
Orders: 1.800.835.4993
www.gibbs-smith.com

Designed by Black Eye Design
Printed and bound in Canada
Gibbs Smith books are printed on either recycled, 100%
post consumer waste, or FSC certified papers.

Library of Congress Cataloging-in-Publication Data

King, Bart, 1962-
  Pocket guide to boy stuff / Bart King ; illustrations by
  Chris Sabatino. — 1st ed.
     p. cm.
  ISBN-13: 978-1-4236-0574-4
  ISBN-10: 1-4236-0574-8
  1. Teenage boys—Life skills guides—Juvenile liter-
  ature. 2. Teenage boys—Conduct of life—Juvenile
  literature. 3. Teenage boys—Anecdotes. I. Sabatino,
  Chris. II. Title.
  HQ775.K568 2009
  646.700835'1—dc22

                                        2008036614

This book makes mention of some activities that could
theoretically carry an element of risk. Readers naturally assume all legal responsibility for their actions.

CONTENTS

★★★

This book is dedicated to Suzanne Taylor . . . after all, it was HER idea.

★★★

Featuring favorite activities and cool stuff from *The Big Book of Boy Stuff*.

Introduction

Boys' Introduction

Maybe someone gave you this book as a gift. Maybe you don't want to read it. Maybe you think this book stinks.

Think again.

Read this book. You're going to like it.

Trust me!

Adult Introduction

As a teacher, I find it gratifying to see a student read a book he really *wants* to read. In fact, if you've ever wondered what makes one teacher high-five another, discovering a book that a reluctant reader finds appealing ranks right up there. (Getting a good parking spot rates a distant second.)

Considering what makes a book irresistible is how I came to write *Boy Stuff*. Is it silly? Yes. Gratuitous? You betcha. Naturally, I hope that this volume encourages the act of reading. But it's also my aim that a boy (or girl!) can find something worthwhile to do, to laugh at, or to think about in the following pages.

Will this solve our nation's literacy problems? Of course it will! Now then, isn't there a special someone you should give this book to?

9

Activities!

So, you're looking for something to do, huh? Well, you've come to the right place. The best kind of fun is the fun you make on your own. Remember when you were a little ankle-biter and you'd make a fort by throwing a blanket or some old sheets over the couch? Or the time that you tied a garbage bag around yourself and slid down the snow-covered hill? And remember when you made your own jet plane and flew to Timbuktu?

Before reading on, you must promise to use the following outstanding activities

for good, not evil. Do you promise? Are your fingers crossed? Are your eyes crossed? Okay, then take a look below! I have listed the activities from the easiest to the most challenging.

★ *THE MOST DANGEROUS DANCE IN THE WORLD!* Be careful when you learn the traditional Polish dance called the *zbojnicke* (djeh-BOHJ-nick-ee). That's the one where the man swings an axe in circles above the ground and the woman has to jump over it, duck under it, and basically look out. Then *she* takes the axe!

11

I Am an Idiot

This is probably the stupidest activity of all time. Because of this, it always cracks me up.

YOU NEED: to have the alphabet memorized

Try to say the alphabet without moving your lips or your tongue at all. No cheating! Whenever I do this, every letter sounds exactly the same; try it for yourself. (Hey, I said I would start with the easy stuff. If you find this activity too challenging, you may want to put this book down and go eat a Popsicle.)

Treasure Hunt in the Couch

For those on the lookout for spare change and cracker crumbs!

YOU NEED: a couch or sofa

If you are tough enough to brave the sight of lint, small toys, dirt, and crumbs, you might make enough money to buy a candy bar by playing this game.

Here's what you do: Put on coveralls and plastic gloves. (Protective eyewear is optional.) Drag a garbage can over to the sofa. Now lift up one of the sofa cushions. Careful! You never know what kind of filthy varmint might be hiding down there! There could be cockroaches, or even that annoying kid from down the block.

Anyway, keep pulling up the cushions. As you find disgusting pieces of rancid and dried-out food, throw them out. If you find any clothes you've been missing, put them in the laundry. If that annoying neighbor kid is down there, send him home pronto! And finally, the treasure: nickels, dimes, quarters, maybe even dollars! Heck, maybe there's a credit card down there! I just did this, and I made $1.35, so try this amazing game every few months or so and see what you come up with.

Talk the Cop Talk, Walk the Cop Walk

Looking for official police officer activities? Use the following information.

FOR ACTIVITY 1, YOU NEED: this book!

FOR ACTIVITY 2, YOU NEED: Krazy Glue; any box with a lid

Activity 1

You've probably noticed that police officers have lots of codes and lingo that they use. Codes are not only practical, but they sound cool too. For example, if an officer is radioing in a suspicious license plate, they don't say, "Run a check on license *174 DBP.*" The problem is that some letters sound like other things; in this license, D sounds like B and P, which could mess things up. *("One-Adam-12, did someone pee on your license plate?")*

Instead, the officer might say, "Run a check on 174 Delta Bravo Papa." This is cool cop talk that keeps things sensible! Here is the cop talk alphabet:

ALPHA, BRAVO, CHARLIE, DELTA, ECHO, FOXTROT, GOLF, HOTEL, INDIA, JULIET, KILO, LIMA, MIKE, NOVEMBER, OSCAR, PAPA, QUEBEC, ROMEO, SIERRA, TANGO, UNIFORM, VICTOR, WHISKEY, X-RAY, YANKEE, ZULU

Use these words to spell things out ("Please be advised that I would like some *Golf-Uniform-Mike* now") as well as for general silliness. ("Dad, take cover! We have a *Zulu alert!* Repeat, a *Zulu alert!*")

Activity 2

Detecting fingerprints is one of the most important police tools there is. If you have ever wanted to do this yourself, here's what you do.

Get a small box with a lid (a shoebox works great). Pour a small puddle of Krazy Glue on a piece of foil or waxed paper (or anything.) Put that at one end of the box. Put the item you want to check for fingerprints at the other end of the box. This method will work best on hard, smooth items: anything glass, metal, or hard plastic will work, like a mirror or a knife blade. Make sure the lid is on tight. Leave the box in the sun for four to five hours. Come back and check for prints! (The molecules from the glue will get stuck to the greasy fingerprints!)

If you want to compare the prints to a suspect's, have your suspect push their finger on an inkpad and roll their finger one time on a sheet of white paper.

Kung Fu Egg

It's time to use lightning-quick reflexes on an egg!

YOU NEED: an egg; a piece of aluminum foil; a glass; a playing card

Don't use a hard-boiled egg for this trick; it's more exciting if you don't! The setup for this activity just takes a moment. You just need to make a foil-ring platform to hold up the egg. Cut or tear a rectangular piece of foil and make a ring with it that will support the egg with its fat end down.

Now fill the glass about ⅔ of the way with water. Put the playing card over the glass. Finally, set the foil ring and egg in the center of the card.

17

Practice a few good kung fu yells and moves! Scream, chop, and kick! Finally, approach the egg. With a show of great concentration, reach out your hand and quickly and sharply flick the card hard, so that it shoots off the glass. The egg will sink into the water, and it won't even break!

★*DON'T TRY THIS ACTIVITY WITH AN OSTRICH EGG!* Ostriches lay the biggest eggs of any bird. One of their eggs could support your weight if you stood on it, and its contents are equal to 24 chicken eggs!

Screen Message

Use your TV as a chalkboard!

YOU NEED: a TV in a room that gets dark; a strong flashlight

Okay, make sure that the room the TV is in is *totally* dark and that the TV is turned off. Take the flashlight and push it up against the top left corner of the TV.

18

Now turn the flashlight on and, without removing it from the screen, write your name by sliding the flashlight on the screen. Don't go too fast! When you're done, turn the light off and step back. Your name will be in lights!

Now get up next to the TV and put your hand on the screen. With your other hand, take the flashlight and start shining it all over the screen. Don't move the beam too fast; do this for no less than two minutes. (Longer for better effect.) Once you've done the above, turn off the flashlight and remove your hand. You will see a dark image of it on the screen, while the screen glows behind it!

Pet on a Leash

Don't just swat those big houseflies! Catch them!

YOU NEED: a plastic container with a lid; some thread

Don't you hate it when one of those gigantic houseflies gets inside and starts divebombing your head when you're trying to do something important, like take a nap? Well, instead of just swatting the big galoot, why not do something more creative?

Wait until the fly goes to a window (or any flat surface.) Take a tupperware container that your parents don't mind you using and trap the fly under it! (You've got to be a little fast and a lot patient.) Then slide the lid under the container without lifting up the edges much, so the fly doesn't escape.

Seal the lid on. Don't worry, the fly won't suffocate; that's because you are going to put it in the freezer! The temperature will fall so quickly, the fly will be "knocked out" in a little while. Smart people call this "cryostasis." (I call it "really cold.")

Check the fly in about 10–15 minutes. If it looks unconscious, have your thread ready, and open up the container. Acting carefully and quickly, tie a knot with the thread around one of the fly's legs. Don't pull it too tight; you don't want to be cruel! (Make sure to wash your hands well once you are done with this; a fly can have millions of germs on its body.)

Unroll a few feet of the thread, and cut the other end. Put it under something heavy, so the insect can't fly away when it wakes up. Then wait for a while. The fly will come to and try to fly. Then it will reach the end of the thread. It's your pet!

When you are done playing with your fly, take it outside, reel it in a ways, and cut the thread as close to it as you can. Set it free!

Monster Teeth

These are the perfect thing to do if you are babysitting some young kids and want to scare them!

YOU NEED: an orange; a knife (careful!); some kitchen scissors

Cut an orange from top to bottom into halves. (Be careful; if you cut your finger off, this isn't as much fun.) Then cut the halves in half from top to bottom, so that you have four quarters of an orange.

Peel one of the sections. Then take the orange peel and cut it lengthwise down the middle. *Not all the way!* Leave about ½ inch at each end.

Now you need to make the teeth. About every ¼ inch on both sides of your first cut, make a ¼-inch cut with your scissors. (These little cuts should be toward the edge of the orange peel.)

You're ready! Turn the orange peel inside out, put it under your lips, and go look in the mirror. *Most excellent!*

Shooting the Airball

The coolest thing that you've never done!

YOU NEED: 2 heavy nonflammable objects; a blow-dryer; a Ping-Pong ball

Take the blow-dryer and place it between your two heavy objects. (Don't block the blow-dryer's intake vent with either of these.) Point the air drier straight up. Then plug it in and turn it on to its highest setting. Now take your Ping-Pong ball and place it in the airstream about a foot over the drier. Amazing! It should stay suspended in the air. If it doesn't, try placing it farther up or down in the airstream. As gravity pulls down, the air pushes up, and the ball stays in the middle!

Now if you want to shoot your air ball, just go get the peashooter that you can design in the Weapons chapter, page 251, and have at it!

The Primitive Phone

Yeah, you could use a real phone, but why?

YOU NEED: a couple of cans; some string or a long garden hose; 2 funnels; some duct tape

I'm going to assume that you have probably already made a phone-line by tying a piece of string between two cans. That is a really primitive phone, where the sound waves of your voices follow the string to the cans.

Let's take it a step further. If you have an old garden hose (the longer, the better) lying around that your family doesn't want anymore, have your parents cut off the metal ends with a hacksaw. Stick one funnel in each end and tape them in place.

If you put one funnel up to your mouth and the other up to your ear, you can say something and then hear it a second or two afterward. Now give one end to your friend and have him go out of sight. Have secret conversations! Use the hose as the way to communicate with your hideout!

Aren't You Glad You Use Sundials?

Some people can tell the time by just looking at the sun, but even when I wear sunglasses, I can never see its numbers!

YOU NEED: a pencil; clay or Playdoh; a flowerpot; a wooden stick (like a chopstick)

You know not to look at the sun, but there are ways to tell the time from the sun *without* looking at it! People have used sundials for thousands of years to tell time. To learn one way, take a blob of clay and stick it in the bottom of your flowerpot. Then put your stick into the clay so that it stands straight up. It should stick up about 3 inches over the rim of the flowerpot; if it doesn't, get a longer stick or a smaller pot!

To "set" your sundial, you need to put it in a place where the pot will be in the sun all day. Find a good area for it; once you set it, don't move it again. Now, at the top of every hour, make a mark on the edge of the pot where the stick's shadow is. Write down what time it is on the edge at that spot!

It may take a couple of days to get all the hours marked, but once you have, your sundial will be a pretty reliable clock that you made yourself!

★*IF YOU EVER* make a sundial in the classic shape, make sure that the piece that casts a shadow is pointing due north. Use a compass or just point it at the North Star.

Messin' with the Homeys on the Three~way

This works best if one of your friends calls you. You can have a three-way conversation with just one person! This is a great way to kill some time and have some laughs. Although it sounds simple, it works like a charm, and once you start doing it, you can't stop!

YOU NEED: a regular phone; some acting ability

Your friend Ty calls you up and you're talking with him. Suddenly, your friend hears *somebody else* in the room with you. This new person doesn't seem to like Ty very much. From his end of the phone, Ty can hear the person who is with you say, *"Is that Ty? I need to talk to that jerk! He owes me money!"*

Naturally Ty wants to know who is there, but you just apologize for the interruption and keep talking. You might even tell the person in the room with you, "Look, it's not even Ty, okay? Just take it easy."

Of course, *you* are that other person in the room. To make it seem like someone else is there, all you have to do is turn the phone receiver away from your mouth and extend your arm all the way away from you. Now turn your head in the opposite direction of the phone and yell out your comments. Don't try to disguise your voice very much; just yell.

This works best if you do your yelling while Ty is saying something on the other line. Then quickly pull the phone back in and speak in a conversational tone.

If you think this is too simple to work very well, *try it*. It works like a charm!

Land of Tattoos

Tattoos are fun, but the problem is that you eventually get tired of them. This is why many adults who get tattoos either have the tattoo removed or keep getting more and more of them. Temporary tattoos are the way to go, but sticker tattoos are for wussies. Here are a couple of ways to get tattoos that will be your own design.

Sun Tattoos

Here comes the sun . . . and it's going to tattoo you!

YOU NEED: the sun; a permanent marker;
some sunscreen (optional)

METHOD A

Use a permanent marker to draw your
design on your belly, arms, legs, or back.
After the ink dries, put on sunscreen and
go have fun in the sun!

When you are done in the sun, soak some
cotton balls in rubbing alcohol and clean
off the marker ink. Voilà! There is a light
tattoo of your design! If you don't like it,
just go out in the sun some more and tan

over it! If you do like it, keep using marker on the design before going outside.

METHOD B

Create your design, and then draw it on your body with a sunscreen that has a high SPF number (30 and higher should work.) This method is easier to clean up after, although it is harder to draw the tattoo with.

Painted Tattoos

Just paint yourself and then hang out with some bikers!

YOU NEED: tempera paints (dry or wet); small bowls; lotion; cotton swabs or paintbrushes

If your tempera paints are wet, just put the different colors into different bowls. If they are dry, put some lotion in the bowls first, then mix the tempera paint color into it until it looks right.

Once the colors are ready, start painting yourself! You can use cotton swabs, paintbrushes, or your fingers to make designs. Cover your face completely with designs! Go native! Take pictures!

Freak Face

If you want to get absolutely wacky and you don't mind a little discomfort, try this!

YOU NEED: school-supply-style rubber cement; a crazy attitude; a willingness to have a red face for an hour or so after the activity

WARNING: DO NOT USE KRAZY GLUE, MODEL GLUE, OR ELMER'S GLUE FOR THIS ACTIVITY; USE RUBBER CEMENT ONLY.

This should be done in front of a mirror. Take the rubber cement. Apply a 1- to 2-inch band of it around your mouth, starting about ¼-inch from your lips. Let it dry a little. Now turn your lips inside out and stick them to the rubber cement. You will be amazed at the effect!

The rubber cement will stick to itself, your lips will be flipped, and you will look completely insane! Try not to talk while you wander around scaring people, or your lips will come undone. When you're done, gently pry your lips off your face and wash with soap and warm water.

If you don't want to do your whole mouth the first time you try this, just do your upper or lower lip to get a feel for it.

Secret Message Man

If you don't know how to write in invisible ink yet, here's how to do it!

YOU NEED: white paper; a mirror

METHOD A (EASY)

Get out a pad of paper and stand in front of a mirror. Practice writing while looking at the message in the mirror. It will seem weird at first because you will be writing backward; the mirror reverses everything!

If you find this too hard, just sit down to write. Write your message in regular writing first. Then carefully write it on a separate sheet in reverse! Remember that *everything* must be reversed; the last word of the sentence becomes the first. The word is spelled backward and written backward. A *d* should look like a *b*. Once you're done writing your secret message, nobody will be able to read it . . . except for someone who holds it up to a mirror (or who is dyslexic!).

If this gives you trouble, take a piece of paper and rub a layer of dark crayon or pencil lead on it. Then take another sheet of paper, set it on the colored sheet, and write with a ballpoint pen or sharpened pencil. The message's reverse imprint will show up on the back.

METHOD B (NOT HARD)

YOU NEED: a raw potato

Take the potato and cut it in half. Using the cut end, write a message on the bathroom mirror. (I've always liked messages

like *"Prepare to die!"*) The message is invisible. BUT when someone takes a shower next, the message will show up on the mirror because of the steam! Whoohoo!

METHOD C (NOT MUCH HARDER)

You need: lemon juice (or milk); a small glass or jar; a cotton swab; white paper

First, pour the liquid into your glass. *Mmmm, lemony!* Now just dip the cotton swab into the liquid and then use the swab to write your message on the white paper. Re-dip the swab into the liquid if it dries out.

Let your writing dry out; it should become invisible. When you are ready to read the message, hold it up to a strong light or fire; the words will magically appear! Another way to get the message to appear is to have an adult use an iron at low temperature to "iron" the piece of paper.

Because lemon juice and milk darken when heated, the message shows up.

★*IF YOU EVER* want to read *someone else's message* in a sealed envelope, spray the envelope with hair spray. It works pretty well!

The Snorer

Re-create the adventure of snoring while still awake!

YOU NEED: a pocketknife; 1 piece of wood about 8 inches long, 2 inches wide, and ¼-inch thick; some string

If you have ever wanted to imitate the sound a snoring person makes, this is your lucky day! Take your pocketknife out and cut notches into the side edges of the wood. Then whittle the end to a point and bore or cut a hole there that you can run some string through. Tie the string off and leave about 3 feet to use as a handle. Then take it outside and spin it around your head in a circle. It should sound like a lumberjack in a coma!

★*FOR A PERSON TO SNORE,* gravity must pull down parts of the mouth and throat, which makes them vibrate. Astronauts report that in outer space, nobody snores.

Intruder Alert

How to make your own burglar alarm.

YOU NEED: wood glue

> *ALARM A:* 4 small blocks of wood; 2 small cans; some marbles

> *ALARM B:* screw eye or an L-shaped metal bracket; a bell; some string; a staple gun; a piece of stiff wire

Here are two different ways to warn yourself that an intruder is coming in your

room. Whether it's little Timmy from down the street or a mean guy with a big knife, it's nice to have advance warning!

METHOD A

For the first method, glue or screw the blocks of wood onto the door as the illustration shows. Make sure that 1) They are wide enough to hold the cans, and 2) One can is high and close enough to tilt its marbles into the other one. Make sure you get this right!

40

Once your mounts are set, screw in the screw eye. Run a tightly wound string around the doorknob, through the screw eye and into the upper can (which has marbles in it). You may want to put additional blocking around the upper can so that it doesn't simply fall off its mount when pulled by the string.

METHOD B

The second method is even easier. Screw your L-shaped metal bracket into the wall near the door. Hang your bell from it with the string. Staple a piece of stiff wire (like from a coat hanger) so that it lines up with the bell. *Voilà!* When the door opens, the bell is rung and you can be out the window before your mom can set down the milk and cookies!

Fort Building

You've made forts out of the usual pillows and cardboard boxes. Now it is time for the ultimate fort!

41

YOU NEED: newspaper

GODZILLA: grocery bags; tape

IGLOO: 100 or more empty, clean milk jugs; duct tape

Godzilla-style Fort

Take about a dozen sheets of newspaper and crumple them into paper balls. (Don't squish them too tightly.) Now fill a paper bag about ¾ of the way up with the paper balls. Make sure to fill it evenly, but don't wad them down into the bag.

Now neatly fold the top of the paper bag over and tape it shut. You should now have a large, light block. Make about ten more of these and start building. These are perfect for making large structures that you want to walk through and destroy, like King Kong or Godzilla!

Igloo-style Fort

To do this, you'll need a lot of plastic jugs . . . like, 100 or more. If your neighborhood recycles (like they should!), it will be easy to get some jugs from your neighbors. Make sure to wash them out so your igloo doesn't stink.

Take 20 of the milk jugs and make a circle with them. The tops should face inward, the ends should face outward. Then remove 4 or 5 of the jugs from one spot. (This will be the bottom of your door.) Tape the jugs that are left in the semi-circle together with duct tape. If you want a huge igloo, make the circle bigger. If you want a smaller igloo, start with 15 jugs.

Now, put another row of jugs on top of the first row. But bring it in a little bit, so that this row comes inward toward the inside of the circle. Tape them together and leave room for the door. Keep going for 5 or so rows. Each row should come inward and use less jugs than the one before it.

When you get to the 6th or 7th row, close over the top of the door. When you get to the very top, just tape that last jug in place, and be cool in your igloo. *Ice, ice, baby!*

★*IF YOU DECIDE* to tear the igloo down later, just untape and recycle it!

Follow~Up Activity

Are you kidding me? You want a follow-up activity for a chapter called "Activities"? That would be "Hyper-Activity"!

44

Experiments!

"Back in the day," we used to experiment with Life Savers. We would get some mint "Wint-O-Green" Life Savers, go into a closet, and close the door. We would then chomp down on the Life Savers with our teeth and watch the colored lights flash in each others' mouths! We didn't know that we were seeing something called "triboluminescence" (tri-bo-loom-in-es-ens)—we just knew it looked cool. If you want to spare your teeth, just put the Life Savers in a plastic sandwich bag, go in the closet, and hit them with a hammer.

Try the same thing with a Curad strip bandage; don't chew on it, just wait for your eyes to adjust to the dark, then grab the bandage's tabs and yank them open. You'll see a flash of light!

Now it's time to get out your white laboratory coat, Russian accent, and test tubes,

46

because we are going to have a few experiments around here!

The following experiments are all pretty simple, with the easiest ones listed first. And remember, an experiment does not always work the first time. Think about what you did, check the instructions, and experiment again. That's why they're called *experiments!* Sometimes you have to experiment until you get it right.

★ *HERE IS THE ONLY MATH EQUATION YOU WILL FIND IN THIS BOOK:*

$$111,111,111 \times 111,111,111 = 12,345,678,987,654,321$$

It's Different for Girls

Girls and boys are different in many mysterious ways.

YOU NEED: 1 male human *(over eleven years old; ten might work);* 1 female human *(over eleven years old; ten might work);* 2 lip gloss or chapstick or lipstick containers *(don't worry, nobody has to put it on)*

A simple experiment! Have your boy and girl volunteers kneel on the floor. Make sure that their legs are together.

Now, have both of them bend forward and put their elbows up against their knees. Their forearms should extend forward from the knees, with the palms flat against the floor. (Their legs should still be together.)

Place the lip gloss containers (or whatever you're using) upright at the end of their fingers.

Okay, now you're ready. Have both of them now kneel up straight with their legs still together. Have them clasp their hands behind their backs, above their waists.

Now tell them this: *"Keeping your arms and legs in their positions, lean forward, knock the lip gloss over with your nose, and return to the kneeling-up position."*

Watch them! The odds are very high that the girl can do it. The odds are very high that the boy can't!

The reason this happens is because girls tend to have more body weight in the lower half of their bodies than boys do. They can balance better! Next in this chapter are two other balancing experiments. (You can easily do them as magic tricks.)

Other Strength and Balance Experiments!

These don't require girls.

Stand Up

Have your subject stand with his feet together, four foot-lengths from a wall. Have him lean in to the wall with his hands at his sides, so that his forehead is on the wall. Now tell him to stand up straight. He can't!

Weak in the Knees

Tell your volunteer that in a moment he will be unable to lift his right knee while standing on his left leg. You will not interfere or touch him in any way.

Have this person stand with the outside edge of his left foot against a door or wall. Now tell him to put his left shoulder against the wall. After the person has done this, wave your hand over his right knee and say your magic words. *"Great Googly-Moogly!"* Tell the person to keep his left foot and shoulder against the wall and to lift his right knee. He can't. It's magic! (Plus, it can't be done!)

You Can't Make Me

For this experiment, find someone who is stronger than you. (I know, it's not easy.) Challenge them to a strength contest.

Grab your head! Seat yourself on the floor and put your open hand on top of your head, spreading your fingers as wide as you can. Now tell your opponent to try to lift your arm up so that it isn't on your head anymore. He cannot make any quick moves (or kick you or pull from an angle), he can only pull straight up. He can't do it, even if he actually picks you up! *You're stronger!*

Strength-Sucker

Tell your volunteer that you can take away all of his strength with one finger. First, have him sit back in a chair. Tell him to relax, to totally relax. Have him fold his arms and tell him to keep them folded. Step forward, sneakily put the toes of your shoes against his toes. Lean forward, say your magic words (I still like *Great Googly-Moogly!*) and gently but firmly press your finger against his forehead.

Tell him to rise. *He cannot.* Tell him to stand up! *He cannot!* It is impossible to stand up if you are leaning back in your chair, and can't use your arms, and can't move your feet (unless the person cheats and slips out the side.) But he didn't know that! Nice work!

Opposites Attract

Static electricity can make water bend!

YOU NEED: an inflated balloon; a sink with running water; a wool sweater

This is so basic, it's ridiculous. Blow up your balloon and tie it with a knot. Turn on the tap water in the sink. Don't turn it up high; keep the water stream small. Now push the balloon near the running water. Nothing happens! Now rub the balloon on the wool sweater. *Really* rub it! When you're done, push the portion of the balloon you were rubbing toward the running water. Don't get too close, because you'll see that the water is more than happy to help! That's right, the water stream will bend as it tries to get at the balloon! Basically, the static electricity in the balloon (which is negatively charged) is attracting the positively charged part of the water.

NOTE: *IF THE BALLOON GETS WET, ALL CHARGES ARE LOST. DRY IT OFF COMPLETELY AND TRY AGAIN.*

Jumping Beans, Swimming Raisins

I don't know about other dried fruits, but raisins are great swimmers! This is an easy experiment with a fun result.

YOU NEED: any cold, clear carbonated drink: clear soda, mineral water, and tonic water all work; a glass or jar; a handful of raisins

Pour your drink into the glass. Bubbly! Now put a handful of raisins in the glass. They sink! Of course, that's because raisins are heavier than water. Wait . . . they're rising! They're at the top! Now they're going down again . . . *Dive, dive, dive!*

What happens? The raisins are initially heavier than the liquid, but as they sink, they get coated with bubbles. The bubbles form a "life preserver" for the raisins and raise them to the top! There the bubbles burst, and the raisin sinks again. The show is over when the bubbles run out!

EXTRA TWIST: Try turning this into a magic trick! Do the experiment the same way, but when the raisins sink the first time, start saying spells and acting like a spazz to get them to rise. (By the way, this trick also works with plastic pushpins.)

EXTRA, EXTRA TWIST: Try doing the same trick with small, round pieces of Silly Putty. It should work! Now try this: If you put a ball of Silly Putty into water, it will sink. But if you shape your Silly Putty like a boat, it floats!

Journey to the Apple's Core

Tell a spectator what you're going to do and watch their eyes widen!

YOU NEED: a piece of paper; a knife; an apple; a cutting board

Fold the piece of paper once and set the blade of the knife into the fold. You are now going to cut the apple in half, without cutting the paper at all!

Put the apple on the cutting board. Set the knife blade on top of the paper and begin pushing it down on the apple. *(Don't saw it; just push carefully down.)* After you cut through the apple, check out the paper: It's still in one piece!

Beware the Deadly Straw

Sure you can suck liquids through a straw, but straws are also very dangerous!

YOU NEED: plastic straws; an uncooked potato

This is a *fun* experiment to do as a magic trick! Just take the potato and try to stab it with a straw. The straw will bend and maybe stab into the potato a little bit *if you're lucky.*

Now say a magic word *(Hottentot tatertot!)* and hold your thumb over the hole at the end of the straw while you stab the potato with the other end. It should go right into the potato. The farther you push it in, the stronger the straw will get; as the air is trapped inside, the straw gets compressed, making the straw more powerful!

Money Laundering

I did this experiment in a Mexican restaurant with salsa. It was *muy caliente!*

YOU NEED: vinegar and/or salsa; salt; a bowl; dirty coins, preferably pennies; a towel or rag

This is an interesting experiment to do with your money. Just put two cups of vinegar and ½ cup of salt in a bowl and stir them together. Take some dirty, filthy, disgusting pennies and throw them in the mix. If you watch them carefully, you will see them grow shinier before your eyes! Once they're clean, just rinse them in water, dry them, and spend them!

If you want to see something *really* amazing, do the above experiment, but after you put the pennies in the vinegar, put a clean iron nail in with them. Wait for 15 minutes, and the nail will be coated with copper, while the pennies are perfectly clean!

If you use salsa instead of vinegar, throw the coins in and leave them for a little while. The "hotter" the salsa is, the less time they need. What happens is that the acid in the salsa or vinegar sort of "burns" the dirt right off of the coins. This is the same thing that happens if you get some of it in your eyes: It hurts like crazy! The weird thing is, even though salsa burns the heck out of your eyes, you put it in your stomach! The acid that is already in your stomach is much more powerful, so there is no harm done.

I Am Iron Man

You've got a lot of heavy metal in your body, and you don't even know it!

YOU NEED: any breakfast cereal that has "100 percent iron" or "reduced iron" or "iron"; a plastic bowl; water; any magnet that you can hold in your hand and stir with

Your body contains many different metals. One of the most important of these is iron. This is the same metal that you sometimes see rusting; it is in buildings, cars, and *you*.

To prove this, pour cereal into a bowl, then add water. Let the cereal get soggy. Then take the magnet and start stirring the cereal with it. You're going to have to stir a lot; if you have a younger brother or sister, try to trick them into helping you. (It might take up to 30 minutes of stirring to make this work!)

After stirring for a while, check your magnet. You should start to see small black particles forming on it. *Keep going! You will get more! You'll be rich!* Actually, you'll just have a lot of iron. Those small black particles are pieces of metal. You don't usually notice them when you're eating food because they're so small. They have to be small for you to digest them. Believe it or not, there is gold in your body too!

★*OUTER SPACE METAL!* The next time you go to the beach, bring along that magnet. Once you get there, tie the magnet to a string and walk around, dragging it through the sand behind you. The magnet will collect metal particles as you walk. The coolest thing is that about 20 percent of those particles are from meteors!

I Am the Strongest Man in the World (Part I)

Amaze your friends with your strength! Baffle your enemies with your putty!

YOU NEED: Silly Putty; a hammer, rubber mallet, or any heavy, flat object

Roll your Silly Putty into a ball. Put it on something that can take a good blow like a cutting board or a smooth concrete surface. Now hand the hammer or mallet to one of your friends. Tell him to hit the Silly Putty and try to flatten it in one stroke! Your friend will hit it. Nothing. *Try it again!* Nothing. (Even just using the palm of your hand will do as long as the Silly Putty is hit with a fast, sharp blow.)

Call your friend a wimp. Push down on the Silly Putty with your finger and squish it. *Easy!*

The reason this happens is because Silly Putty is actually not a solid, it's a liquid. It reacts differently to slow pressure than it does to hard, sudden pressure. This is the same reason why water feels differently when you do a belly flop off of the high dive than it does when you take a bath.

I Really Am the Strongest Man in the World (Part II)

You won't believe that this will work. It will!

YOU NEED: 10 people; 1 wall

Okay, there don't have to be 10 people, but that's a good number to use. Have your volunteers get in a row by height, with the shortest volunteer at the end of the line, facing you. (This person must be tall enough to reach your shoulders without jumping around to do it.) Make sure that the people are all spaced correctly and aren't cheating.

Tell these people to place their hands on the shoulders of the person in front of them. On your signal, they are to all push on the shoulders of the person in front of them. But even their combined strength will not be enough to push you against the wall!

Now you turn around and face the wall, extend your arms, and put them in front of you on the wall, palms against the wall, fingers pointing straight up. The shortest person then places his hands on your shoulders.

Now tell them to push with all their power. They will huff and puff, but they shouldn't be able to move you! They may fall, but you will stand!

(This is because all the energy they push with only gets as far as the person in front of them. This is called "inertia." As long as you can hold off the person right behind you, you'll be all right.)

Rice Jar Driver

The golf ball will rise! I command it to rise!

YOU NEED: 1 golf ball (or other round object about that size); a jar with lid; uncooked rice

Put the golf ball at the bottom of the jar and then fill the jar with rice. Leave about 1½ inches at the top. Screw on the lid of the jar and shake the jar from side to side. Shake it some more (not up and down, but side to side) while saying your magic words. Now watch the golf ball rise to the surface!

Some people say the *rice is heavier, which moves the golf ball up.* This is not true; a golf ball weighs more than a container of rice the same size. But the rice likes to settle together, and until the golf ball is out of the way, it can't do that, so it pushes the ball up!

The Yolk's in You

If you've ever wanted to see an egg get sucked into a bottle with a bizarre "slurp," this is your experiment!

YOU NEED: a funnel; an empty bottle with a semi-wide mouth (salad dressing bottles are perfect); 1 hard-boiled egg, peeled; water; a tea kettle; a potholder

This experiment happens very quickly! Put the funnel in the mouth of the salad dressing bottle. Put the egg next to the bottle.

Now, boil enough water to fill the bottle. When the water is ready, carefully pour it into the bottle. Take out the funnel and swirl the bottle around a bit. Now, pour the water out and place the egg on the top of the bottle. SLURP!

Now that the egg is in the bottle, what made it go in? Well, hot things expand and cool things contract. The bottle's air was hot, but it was rapidly cooling down and contracting when you put the egg over its only entrance. The bottle had no choice but to suck the egg in.

Now try getting the egg out! Hold the bottle upside down and blow into it for a while, covering the neck with your mouth. When you remove your mouth, it might come out! (But only if you blow hard enough to create enough pressure inside the bottle to pop the egg back out!)

Hard, Sweet, and Sticky

Although some science teachers use this one in the classroom, it's too good to pass up!

YOU NEED: a pencil; a nail; some string; hot water; an empty jar; 2 cups of sugar; a spoon

Tie the pencil and nail to opposite ends of the piece of string. You want the string to be long enough for the pencil to go across the top of the jar with the nail dangling just above the bottom of the jar. Once you have that set up, put it aside.

Put a quarter-cup of hot water in the jar and mix in your sugar. Stir it well with a spoon. Now put the pencil across the top of the jar and hang the nail into the sugar water. Leave the jar alone for a few days and see what happens.

As the water dries up, the sugar will form crystals on the nail.

★*FOR A TWIST,* add food coloring to your mix so that the crystals are blue or green.

Grape Lightning

Who knew that grapes have a bunch of electricity?

YOU NEED: seedless green grapes; a knife; a microwave oven that you can see into

Take a grape. Remove the stem and cut it in half, but not all the way. Leave a skin attachment between the two halves. Put the grape on a plate facing either up or down. Put it in the *center* of the microwave.

Put the microwave on "high" power and set it for 10 to 40 seconds. Now turn it on and watch! You should see sparks, and maybe even electric arcs between the grape parts! At some point, the grape will split all the way apart. When that happens, stop the microwave, because nothing else will happen after that.

★ *IF YOU PREFER YOUR LIGHTNING WITHOUT FRUIT,* try this. Blow up two balloons and knot them at the mouth. Rub one of them against some wool (like a sweater or a sheep) and the other balloon against a wall. Turn off the lights and bring the balloons together. *Zap!*

68

Rubber Bones

Nothing is funnier than a rubber chicken . . . bone!

YOU NEED: any chicken bone that hasn't been cooked yet; a jar with lid; white vinegar

Clean and dry off the bone and leave it alone for a day or two. Then put the chicken bone in the jar and pour enough vinegar into the jar to cover the bone. Screw the lid back on the jar and leave it alone for a week.

After a week, unscrew the lid, pour the vinegar out, and grab the bone. It's rubbery! You may even be able to tie it into a knot. That's because the vinegar dissolved all the calcium from the bone, leaving it soft. A good trick is to do this with a wishbone, and then ask someone to break it with you. This won't work, of course, but you can act amazed!

You can also do this with an egg instead of a chicken bone. Place the egg in the jar and pour enough vinegar into the jar to cover the egg. Screw the lid back on and watch the eggshell slowly dissolve! The shell will be eaten away after a week, leaving only a squishy egg membrane.

Ooblick's Test of Courage

If you needed a good excuse to waste some perfectly good cornstarch, here it is!

YOU NEED: 1 cup of cornstarch; a bowl; some water

Silly Putty is actually a liquid. But what about cornstarch? Put your cornstarch in a bowl or large pan. It's a solid. Add a little water. Stir it in. It will probably get clumpy. Still a solid. Add a little more water. Stir it in. What happened?

As you add and stir in water, you can get the cornstarch to the point where you're not sure what it is. If it feels sort of like mayonnaise, you have just made ooblick! Ooblick is awesome. Pick up some ooblick in your hand and squeeze it in a ball. Solid! Put it back in the bowl and watch it ooze back like a liquid! Now when you stick your fingers in it, it will squish right through them.

You can keep goofing around with the ooblick, or you can move on to the Test of Courage. If you have a few baking pans, make enough ooblick to cover the bottoms of two or three of them. Take the baking pans holding ooblick outside. Set them a couple of feet apart. Take your shoes off. (You can do this with your shoes on if you prefer.) Now walk through the pans! If you make each step quickly and with force, the ooblick will note your courage and leave you alone. If you chicken out and start gently putting your feet into the pans, the ooblick will stick to you!

★*BECAUSE CORNSTARCH IS SO FINE*, it can also be mixed with white glue to make a home-made version of Silly Putty!

Do Robot Sheep Make Steel Wool?

This is a good way to put some sparkle in your life!

YOU NEED: steel wool; 1 "D" battery

Get a piece of steel wool about the size of your fist. Put it on a baking pan or other metal surface and touch the ends of your battery to the steel wool. The iron in the steel wool should sparkle and light up; this is because iron can burn as long as there is enough oxygen around!

Monster in a Box

A good experiment to run over several days.

YOU NEED: a shoebox; a small flowerpot with soil; tape; cardboard pieces; an uncooked potato, sprouted

Take your shoebox and cut a hole a couple of inches wide at one end. Set your flowerpot at the opposite end of the shoebox to measure how much room to leave for it. Then use your pieces of cardboard to make a simple maze between the flowerpot and the hole.

The maze doesn't have to be fancy; just tape the cardboard pieces to the sides of the box in a simple pattern. Put three or four walls with 3-inch openings in different spots.

Now plant the potato in the soil. This experiment will work faster if you use a sprouted potato. You can then cut off a section with the sprout and plant it, but it doesn't matter if you just use a regular tater.

Water your spud, put the lid back on the box, and leave it in a window with some sunlight for several days. If it is hot and you think the plant is getting dry, take the lid off and water it. Otherwise, leave it alone until you see something coming out the hole at the end of the box! Then lift the lid . . . spooky!

Diaper Tricks

You used to wear them; now it's time to tear them!

YOU NEED: an extra-absorbent disposable diaper; three disposable cups; newspaper

Take a disposable diaper and start tearing it apart over the newspaper. When you peel back the lining, you may discover its "magic crystals," which are scientifically designed to absorb the pee and poop . . . or "moisture!" Pull the crystals out of the lining onto the newspaper, and then pour them into a disposable cup.

Now line up your cups. (Have the cup with the crystals in the middle.) Call in an audience. Pour some water into the first cup, until it's about ¼ full. Then pour the water from the first cup into the second cup, the one with the crystals. (The crystals will now absorb the water and stick to the sides of the cup.) Finally, pretend to pour water from the second cup (now empty) to the third cup. Then look down and pretend you're confused.

"Where'd the water go?" you ask, as you begin turning the second and third cups upside-down, peering into them. But there is no water to be found! Shrug your shoulders and say the magician's favorite words: *"Wa-wa go bye-bye!"*

Flaming Greenbacks!

WARNING: ONLY DO THIS EXPERIMENT WHEN A RESPONSIBLE ADULT IS PRESENT!

This money could burn a hole in your pocket!

YOU NEED: a responsible adult; a dollar bill; salad tongs; rubbing alcohol; dish or bowl; a bigger dish or bowl full of water; matches or a lighter

Perform this experiment near a sink or outside on a concrete surface.

Take a dish or bowl and pour some rubbing alcohol into it. Now mix the alcohol in the bowl with an equal amount of water.

Take your dollar bill and hold it with the salad tongs. Dip the bill into the dish and soak it for a moment in your mixture. Pull it out and hold it away from yourself. Have the responsible adult hold a flame next to the bill.

This is the great part. The dollar bill will catch on fire, but it won't burn! You will see a blue-colored flame surround the dollar, but the water will keep the dollar wet and safe, as the alcohol burns off. In other words, the water will put out the flame that the alcohol begins! (If anyone starts to "freak out" when the bill is surrounded by flame, you can always put the dollar in the big bowl of water or the sink.)

To be sure the bill is "out," put it in the bigger dish full of water before hanging it up to dry.

Follow~Up Activities

1. Rig the roof of your house with a lightning rod. Wire the electricity to go to your bedroom, where you can use it to reanimate dead bodies and also to make toast. Adult supervision is required.

2. Research time travel and then make your own time machine. Use it to travel back in time to answer the most important question that has ever faced the human race: *Where did I lose my pocketknife on September 14, 2002?*

Fireworks and Explosions!

One of the greatest pleasures of life is blowing up an old model of an airplane or a car with some firecrackers! So I'm not going to pretend that fireworks aren't fun, but the fact is that every day some kid blows off his fingers by not following proper safety procedures with fireworks. SO READ THIS NOW:

Important Information

When I was 12, my friends and I were waiting at the bus stop. An older kid started messing around with firecrackers. He would light the firecrackers and throw them in the street. *Bang! Bang!* The rest of us watched.

One of the firecrackers that he lit didn't go off. It just sat in the street, looking innocent. "That one's a dud," I said helpfully.

This kid looked at me and went and got the dud. After he picked it up, the "dud" went off with a nice *"bang!"* in his hand. He screamed (*"Yeow!"*) and started running around like a chicken with its head cut off. "I guess it wasn't a dud after all," I said helpfully.

That kid was lucky. He didn't blow his hand off, but he did get a nasty explosion burn on his hand, and his example taught us all a lesson that day. *There's no such thing as a dud.* Firecrackers and other fireworks are unpredictable. Once a firework has been lit, do not pick it up again unless it has been soaked with water for a long time.

Here are some other safety measures that will save you from injury. *Make sure* there are adults around when you set off fireworks. *Make sure* you are well away from any buildings or plants that could catch fire. *Make sure* there are no dogs or other animals around. *Make sure* you always have buckets of water ready to throw on any spark. Douse sparks immediately and ask questions later. I don't

care if that spark landed on your Aunt Matilda's wig. *Get it wet!*

So let's say you have some legal fireworks, you're with some responsible adults, and you are in a safe area to set them off. (A cinder block in the middle of an empty parking lot or street would be perfect.) Now, move your fireworks supply *50 feet* away from that spot. You don't want all your fireworks going off at once if a spark

Nine of the 50 states don't allow people to use any fireworks at all, so if you live in one of these states, congratulations. You're safe from fireworks! Another nine states allow some fireworks, but do not allow firecrackers. Many cities and counties also have their own fireworks laws, so here's what you must do: *Know and obey the fireworks laws in your area.* For information on the laws in your area, visit the National Council on Fireworks Safety Web site at *WWW.FIREWORKSAFETY.COM.*

lands in there. The screams would be incredible!

What now? Do you have protective eyewear on? You should. Heck, I wear long sleeves, a hat, and gloves too. You can't be too careful! Anyway, now you're ready to light the fuse to some fireworks. Whenever you are lighting a fuse, keep your body away from the firework. Use a long-handled lighter or long match and *reach out* to light the fuse. (I turn my face away from it, too, just in case.) If this seems like overdoing it, just think: a regular little sparkler burns at a heat of 1,000 degrees Fahrenheit!

That's it. Light one item at a time, and have fun!

Your Safety Test

Okay, let's see if you can handle fireworks. Do this: Get a lemon. Cut off a piece of its rind. Now light a candle. Holding the outside of the rind with your fingers, get close to the flame and squeeze the inner parts together. Cool sparks, huh?

Did you burn your fingers? Explode your pancreas? Either way, read the next paragraph carefully.

What Happens if You Don't Follow Safety Rules?

Every year, there are more than 8,000 fireworks injuries brought into hospital emergency rooms. Almost half of those thousands of people will be *kids under the age of 15*. Don't let this happen to you! The parts of the body usually injured are the eyes, hands, head, and face. You will want to use all of those body parts in the future, *so be careful!* Finally, ⅓ of these injuries will come from *illegal* fireworks, so buy the legal kind. They're safer!

★ *SOAK FIREWORKS* completely in water before putting them in the trash.

★ *IF YOU ARE GOING TO STORE FIREWORKS*, put them in a cool, dry place. Tape shut the container they're in, so that no moisture can get inside.

Gunpowder
"The Devil's Invention"

Gunpowder is what made early fireworks go BOOM! But who was the first genius to discover the magical properties of gunpowder? As with so many other things (yo-yos, compasses, cards, kites, pasta), it was an unknown person living in China. About a thousand years ago, this person (probably a cook) accidentally mixed salt-peter (potassium nitrate), sulfur (used to make a fire burn hotter), and charcoal together. BOOM!

The Chinese didn't call this stuff "gunpowder" because guns hadn't been invented yet. They called their invention *huo yao* or the "fire chemical." It didn't take too long for the Chinese to figure out that if they attached bamboo tubes filled with the chemical to arrows, the arrow would go extra fast. After a while, they left the arrow out of the equation since the tubes could launch themselves and create a nice explosion up in the air! The Chinese used their new invention for many celebrations and events.

One Chinese man, Wan-hu, even tried to use these rockets to fly. He set up two big kites with a chair and 42 rockets. *Three, two, one,* TAKE-OFF! There was a loud explosion, and Wan-hu was gone! Was he up in the air? *Nope.* Was he in the ashes that were left where the explosion was? *Yep!* Wan-hu *was* the ashes that were left where the explosion was!

The Chinese used *huo yao* for celebrations and also for exploding arrows and other weapons. But when the Europeans and Arabs got their hands on this explosive powder, they began inventing cannons, guns, and other antisocial devices. This is when it got its nickname, "The Devil's Invention."

But gunpowder has had peaceful uses. Northern Italians were especially inter-ested in fireworks after the famous

traveler Marco Polo brought back firework recipes from the mysterious East for them to use. In 1292, Marco Polo wrote of his firecracker collection: "They burn with such a dreadful noise, they can be heard for ten miles at night . . . it is the most terrible thing in the world to hear for the first time." To this, I say: *"Marco . . . Wusso!"*

In early America, firearms and fireworks were very popular. (Maybe you've heard the line from "The Star-Spangled Banner" about *the rockets' red glare?*) One unusual form of American fireworks was an activity called "Shooting the Anvil." A blacksmith's heavy anvil was set up in an open area. A bag of gunpowder with a fuse coming out was then placed on top of it. The people would then put another anvil on top of the bag, light the fuse, and run away! The colonists had to keep their eyes open, though. After the explosion, the top anvil would fly *way* up in the air, and what goes up could come down on them!

Back in those days, to discourage kids from shooting guns for fun, adults actually encouraged the use of firecrackers as a safe alternative. Boys came up with fun uses for their firecrackers, like attaching them to large weeds to knock them down, sticking firecrackers in tomatoes for juicy explosions, and of course, blowing up their toy soldiers.

Firework Types

There are many different types of fireworks: pinwheels, Roman candles, rockets, squibs, gerbs, and so on. But there are really just two basic elements that most fireworks have in common: They either go *"Boom!"* like a firecracker, or they give off cool lights and sparks like a sparkler. Maybe they do both! You already know about firecrackers. Sparklers, though, are usually made by dipping a stick in a gooey mix of chemicals. Contained in the chemicals is a black powder (a gunpowder type of mix) so that the sparkler burns. Mixed in with the powder are flecks of metal dust, like iron, aluminum, or magnesium. When these get hit with a high temperature, they burn with a bright spark. For example, zinc burns with a green color, while aluminum burns with a white flame.

When you see fireworks going off in the sky ("aerial fireworks"), you can see both of these firecracker and sparkler elements. Aerial fireworks are usually shot out of a cannon-like device called a "mortar." All the ingredients needed for the fireworks are in a shell with a fuse. (The length of the fuse determines how high the fireworks are when they explode.)

When the aerial fireworks go off, you hear a loud BANG first. That sound comes from the explosive in the middle of the shell, which is much like a big firecracker. Then you see the starburst of color coming out of it. (By the way, blue is the hardest color to show with fireworks.) These colored starbursts are really just bigger chunks of the same stuff you find on a sparkler. The *pattern* of these starbursts is decided by how they are placed inside the shell.

If you see more than one explosion from the same firework, the shell may have other shells with different colors or sound-making devices hidden within it.

Different cultures like different aspects of fireworks. The Japanese word for fireworks is *hanabi,* which means "flowers of fire." They like fireworks that give off smoke clouds and star bursts in different colors. In Europe, many people enjoy the *noise* of fireworks the most—you know, that moment when the explosion goes off and you can feel the air press in on your eardrum: BOOM! Sometimes it's so scary, the next thing you know, *Euro-peein'!*

Gunpowder is not usually used much in fireworks anymore. Firecrackers usually have something called "flash powder" in them, which was originally made for photography. But one thing hasn't changed. Boys dig the sound of fireworks, whether they whistle, screech, or bang. (Unless they're duds!)

★*FIRECRACKERS MAKE GOOD FIRE ALARMS!* People have been known to put firecrackers in different parts of the walls and roof of a house while it is being built. That way, if a fire ever breaks out, the firecrackers will go off, waking everyone in the house!

★ *THE LONGEST STRING OF FIRECRACKERS* ever set off was in Hong Kong in 1996. To celebrate the Chinese New Year, a string of firecrackers was lit that took 22 hours to completely explode.

★ *THERE IS A TOWN* in Massachusetts called Fireworks.

Hand Grenades

Hand grenades are the only hand-thrown devices still used by armies. Like most explosions, a hand grenade blows up because of expanding gases. Here are two hand grenade designs that you can use that won't start a fire or blow off your hand!

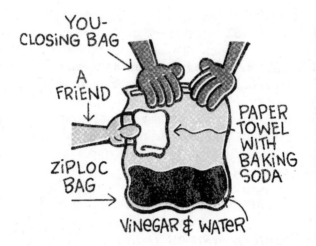

YOU-CLOSING BAG

A FRIEND

ZIPLOC BAG

PAPER TOWEL WITH BAKING SODA

VINEGAR & WATER

Hand Grenade 1

For this grenade, take any small plastic container with a plastic lid, like a small plastic container or a film canister. Fill it ⅓ to ½ with water, then throw a couple of Alka-Seltzer tablets in it. Quickly snap on the lid, and throw it! *Bang!*

Hand Grenade 2

Get a ziplock sandwich bag. (Not the giant freezer bags, but one of the smaller models.) Also, get some vinegar and baking soda, and a paper towel. Then cut a 6-inch square off of your paper towel and put 3 tablespoons of baking soda in the middle of it. Now fold it up.

Over the sink, pour ¾ cup of vinegar and ⅓ cup of warm water into the bag. Now comes the tricky part: You want to put the paper towel into the bag without letting it touch the vinegar! You may want to have someone help you, as they pinch the folded paper towel inside the bag while you carefully zip it tightly.

Once the bag is zipped, take it outside, drop the folded paper towel into the vinegar, shake the bag, and drop it on the ground. You should get a good bang out of it! (If not, try changing the amounts described above; I sometimes skip the warm water part.)

The Dry Ice Boomer

NOTE: THIS ACTIVITY CAN ONLY BE DONE WITH ADULT SUPERVISION AND EYE PROTECTION!

WARNING: DRY ICE IS FROZEN CARBON DIOXIDE. IT IS REALLY COLD! DRY ICE IS USUALLY COLDER THAN −75 DEGREES FAHRENHEIT, SO IF IT TOUCHES YOUR SKIN, YOU'RE IN TROUBLE. IT WILL STICK TO YOU AND CAUSE FREEZING BURNS AND FROSTBITE! ONLY HANDLE IT WITH GLOVES AND SALAD TONGS!

YOU NEED: a 2-liter plastic soda bottle; dry ice; the outdoors; a wrist rocket or sling-shot

This might be the simplest exploding device of all time. If you do it correctly, it is perfectly safe.

Take your *plastic* soda bottle and some dry ice. (Only plastic bottles will work for this. Do not use any other kind of container.) Decide what open, safe area you can use for the explosion. It must be a place where you can stand at a safe distance, and where someone would not unexpectedly come upon the bottle or be disturbed by a loud boom!

Once you are in the area where you are going to explode the container, make sure that everything is in place. *You must be prepared to keep an eye on that bottle for up to half an hour.* Okay, now put some dry ice in the bottle. Add water until the bottle is about ¼ full. Crush the side of the bottle a little. Screw on the lid tightly. Stand back.

The dry ice will go through what is called a "phase change." This means it is changing from a *solid* into a *gas*. As it does so, the gas will expand the bottle outward. Once the crushed part of the bottle fills out, you shouldn't go anywhere near it. If the crushed part of the bottle does *not* expand out, it SHOULD still be safe to approach.

Result

There will be a loud boom and the bottle will burst. If the container does not burst, WAIT! Like I said, it could take 30 minutes for it to blow. Do NOT approach the container; it could go off! If you get impatient and want to leave or try again, shoot rocks at the bottle with your wrist rocket (or throw rocks at it, or shoot it with your BB gun, or pop it with a 20-foot spear, or whatever) until you break its side. THEN (and *only* then) is it safe!

Special Section: M-80s and Cherry Bombs

M-80s and Cherry Bombs are *illegal fireworks*. Both of them have been against the law to possess since 1966, and they are very *unsafe*. Do you want to know why they were outlawed? Because so many kids were blowing their hands and feet off with them. Don't buy them! If you see any, they are probably homemade, and if there is one thing you *don't* want home-made, it's fireworks.

M-80s were originally designed as "military rifle-fire simulators." In other words, they were used in the military for exercises when they needed the *sound* of gunshots. Although M-80s are not as powerful as ¼ stick of dynamite (a lot of people think this), they can hurt or kill someone. M-80s contain 60 times more powder than is legal for a firecracker. Lots of firecracker manufacturers try to make their product sound cool by calling them "M-70s" or "M-90s" or things like this.

As for Cherry Bombs, they are usually round and are often dyed red. Just like with the M-80, you will sometimes see legal firecrackers that are called "Cherry Bomb Type" or some baloney like that. Their makers are just trying to trick you into thinking you're buying the real thing.

Avoid ANYTHING that is labeled something like "Cherry Bomb" or "M-80" to avoid getting ripped off or hurt (or both!)

Nitroglycerin and TNT

Many people think a stick of dynamite is just a really big firecracker. WRONG! Dynamite (or TNT) is very different, and the difference is something called "nitroglycerin."

"Nitrogen" is everywhere; for example, it makes up about 80 percent of the air around you right now. "Glycerin" is a sweet syrup used in foods. In 1847, an Italian named Ascanio Sobrero was experimenting with glycerin in an attempt to find a cure for headaches. He mixed some glycerin with some acid and he ended up with what we now call "nitroglycerin." Ascanio learned that the combination of glycerin and acid is explosive when the glass tube it was in blew up in his face, leaving him badly scarred.

Ascanio was a good man. He tried to keep this terrible new explosive a secret because he was afraid of how it might be used in the wrong hands. But word of the explosive got out. Nitroglycerin was very unstable and dangerous, but that didn't stop people from messing around with it. Ascanio said, "When I think of all the victims killed during nitroglycerin explosions . . . I am almost ashamed to admit to be its discoverer."

A man from Sweden named Alfred Nobel worked at trying to make nitroglycerin safe for use in road-building and mining. It took years of work, and his own brother was killed in an accident with it, but Alfred discovered that if he mixed nitroglycerin with a special kind of dirt and molded it into sticks, it would not explode by itself. He called this invention "dynamite."

Alfred Nobel was an unusual person. His father made guns and explosives for armies. But Alfred was an inventor and poet who spoke 5 languages and thought of himself as a loner. He made a fortune from his invention of dynamite, but like Ascanio Sobrero, Alfred had a conscience. He set up a system of special prizes that would be given out every year to people who make a valuable contribution to the world in science or the arts or for peace. These are called the Nobel prizes, and they have been given out yearly since 1901.

Follow-Up Activity

There is an ultimate weapon so frightening and awful, only a crazy person would ever use it. Because this ultimate weapon is so terrifying to others, it can be used to bring peace to the world. I am, of course, talking about your dad's gas problem. Encourage your dad never to bomb unless he is punishing evildoers or trying to scare a salesperson away from the front door.

Flying Things!

If you're interested in launching something into the air, you've come to the right place!

Turtles

In 456 BC, a very bald man named Aeschylus was minding his own business when a flying turtle hit him in the head, killing him. (Aeschylus was a famous playwright in ancient Greece.) How bald was Aeschylus? He was so bald, an eagle that had caught this turtle flew up and dropped the shelled reptile on a shiny "rock" to break it open. This didn't work. The rock was Aeschylus's gleaming skull, and the turtle's shell didn't break.

Kites

Kites were invented in China 3,000 years ago. These first kites were not for fun and games, however. They were used by soldiers to signal each other from far away. The color and type of kite as well as the way it was flown gave a message to another soldier.

Back then, boys imitated what the grown-ups did. (Oh wait, boys *still* do that!) Since soldiers were "playing" with kites, Chinese boys and girls started doing the same thing. (Hopefully they didn't foul up the army's communications.)

Anyway, kites are cool, but you don't really need this book to learn about them.

I am happy simply to share with you the coolest kite of all time. It doesn't need a string, and it catches on fire! It is . . . the Kite O' Flame!

The Kite O' Flame

When this is done properly, you will get "Oohs!" and "Aahs!" from all who see it!

YOU NEED: a full sheet of newspaper; Scotch tape; 4 people with matches or lighting devices; a cool or cold night; adult super-vision

The idea of the Kite o' Flame is that it will fly up on its own while burning majesti-cally, and then disappear into the air. You have to see it to believe it! There are no strings with this kite; heat rises, and the kite will rise from the heat of its flames. Because of the heat factor, this kite will only work if it is cool or cold out; fly it in the evening, when you can appreciate its effect.

WARNING: BECAUSE OF ITS FLAME, ONLY DO THIS ACTIVITY WITH YOUR PARENTS PRESENT. ONLY FLY THIS KITE IN AN AREA AWAY FROM HOUSES AND PLANTS. A PARKING LOT IS PERFECT.

Take the newspaper and lay it down so that the main crease forms a small moun-tain (not a valley.) Bring the 4 corners together to meet in the middle; try to make the points line up perfectly. Care-fully tape the four corners to each other.

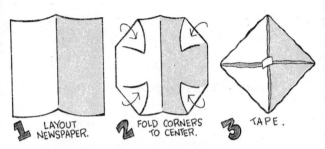

1 LAYOUT NEWSPAPER. 2 FOLD CORNERS TO CENTER. 3 TAPE.

The puffy area of air that you will create is what makes this kite fly. Turn the kite over, then place a person with a match at each of the 4 corners.

Have everyone light their match at the same time. On your command, they should all light the corner they are holding. The kite will begin to slowly rise if you have prepared it properly; you may need to try this a couple of times to get it taped and lit correctly, but it's worth it. The kite does not rise far or go fast, but it is awesome.

★ *THERE ARE COMPETITIVE KITE-FLYING* games in some Southeast Asian countries in which the kites are equipped with sharp edges.

Contestants then try to shred their opponents' kites!

Paper Airplanes

The cool thing about paper airplanes is that they never need batteries. (You can try putting a battery into yours, but they don't usually fly as well.) Since a paper airplane has no engine, its design must take advantage of airflow and wind to keep it in the air. If it doesn't fly as well as you wanted, that just means that you should *experiment* with different adjustments and wing folds and stabilizers and try again.

Plane Construction

When you create your plane, fold on a flat surface. Use good straight folds, no rough edges, and try to make it perfect. It will really pay off.

Plane Flights

Never judge a paper airplane on its first flight! Throw the plane gently, like a dart. Most planes climb and then stall if you throw them too hard. If your plane climbs and then stalls even if you throw gently, try putting more weight on the nose; sometimes just a small piece of paper taped at the nose does the trick.

If the plane turns (or "banks") in either direction, the wings have uneven angles. Check them and refold if necessary.

Some of the terms used in this section include the following:

CREASE: same thing as a fold.

VALLEY: paper's fold looks like a valley, or the letter V.

MOUNTAIN: paper's fold looks like a mountain, an upside-down V.

AIR-TO-GROUND ROCKET: device installed on paper airplanes to eliminate targets, like the annoying neighborhood kid or the barking poodle next door.

ELEVATOR: adjustments that can be made on the back of the plane that adjust its flight. If the elevators are up, the plane's nose will come up. Generally, I make my elevators about ¼ inch deep and about an inch long.

YOU NEED: paper (duh!), standard 8½- by 11-inch sheets; a pen or pencil for marking; a ruler (good for folding and measuring); transparent tape

Hangin' with the Glider

With just a few folds, this may be the fastest plane you can make.

1. Fold the paper in half the long way, open it, and fold the top two corners in so that the edges are right on the center fold.

2. Take the top peak of the triangle that is formed and fold it down to the middle crease. (How far you fold is up to you; I stop at about 1¼ inches from the bottom of the paper.)

3. Now fold the top left and right corners down to the middle crease again just like

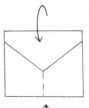

you did in Step 1. Leave a tiny bit of room between them. (A small triangle will be sticking below this.)

111

4. Fold everything down that center crease to make a mountain. (This will make your triangle rise up and fold in half.)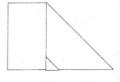

5. You're almost done. Turn your paper so that the pointy end is in your palm. Fold the wings on each side by folding from 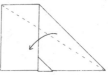 the point to the end and making the top align with the bottom.

6. Once you get that fold, open up the wings so they are flat and even. Give it a slow,

steady throw. I like to tape the middle of the body together to keep it tight.

Bull's-Eye: The Dart

Every boy needs to memorize this design. It is the best version of the most classic paper airplane ever!

1. Fold the paper in half the long way.

2. With the paper like a valley, fold the top corners in so that they align with the middle crease.

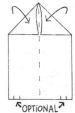

3. OPTIONAL: Now that you have found your top, go to the bottom of the paper. Make a mark from the edge at ½ and 1½ inches from the left and right sides.

4. With those corners folded down, find your new top

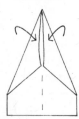

113

corners. Fold these down to
meet the center crease also.

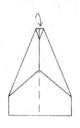

5. The only bad thing about the
dart is, it has a sharp nose
that gets crumpled fast. To
avoid that problem, fold
1 inch of the nose over.

6. Now turn the paper over.
Take the outside edges and
fold them into the center.

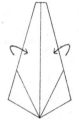

7. Turn it over again. Fold it
right down the center again in the reverse
direction (the oppo-
site way of the first
fold.)

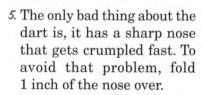

8. Grab the middle
and open the wings. Align the wings so
they are at a 90-degree angle from the
plane's body. Tighten up the body and put
a small piece of tape about 2½ inches in
from the nose to keep the wings together.
Put another small piece of tape where

the wings meet the body to keep it aerodynamic.

Depending on your paper, this design may be too nose-heavy. If your plane goes into dives, look at the marks you made in Step 3. With scissors, make a ¼-inch cut in from those four marks. Fold the paper up to make a flap. These will be the "elevators." These movable flaps will bring any plane's nose up if they are up. (If you've ever sat by the wing in an airplane, now you know what those flaps do.) Now throw the plane again. Awesome! Experiment with different flap settings to make your plane turn and fly differently. The same applies to all other planes.

The Tank

Also known as the Tractor, this is a durable design that can handle a lot of crashing!

1. Take your top left edge and fold it back to the right side.

2. Do the same thing with the other side.

3. Now fold the paper in half.

4. Unfold it, and fold the nose of the paper almost back to the bottom of the folds you have made. (You can fold more or less back depending on whether you want the nose heavier or lighter.)

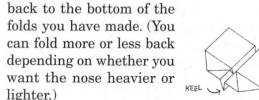

5. Take that fold in the half you made and fold it the other way. You are going to make a keel, which will make a *W* shape when you look at the plane from the front. I make my keel on this model about ⅞ of an inch. Once you get the fold right, you might

want to slightly tape the
front and back to keep it
together.

6. Fold the wings out.

7. Turn the edges of the
wings up. (I usually
fold about ½ inch.)

8. Make any other tape
adjustments needed
to keep that keel
together, then try a
throw. You may want
to add elevators and rudders to the wings
to get the flight path you want.

The Ring of Power!

It's not an airplane. It IS a flying circle!

1. You need a square of paper for starters.

2. Fold it in half diagonally.

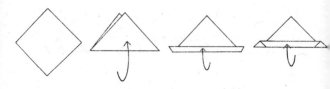

3. Fold a little bit of the folded edge over.

4. Now fold that strip again.

5. Curve the two ends of the folded strip toward each other. Don't fold anything as you go! Now fit or tuck the ends as far as you can into each other. Get it snug.

6. To throw the Ring of Power, pinch the tail end between your thumb and forefinger.

Then hold it up toward your head and push it away from you. A little experimentation will show you the best way to do this.

118

★*DON'T TOUCH IF YOU DON'T KNOW WHAT IT DOES!*
In March 1994, an Aeroflot flight with
75 passengers was flying from Moscow to
Hong Kong. At more than 30,000 feet, the
captain allowed his 11-year old daughter
and 15-year-old son to sit in the pilot's
seat. While there, the pilot's son apparently asked, "May I turn this?" The boy
turned the plane's main control, discon-
necting its autopilot. Nobody noticed this
at first, but the plane then went into a
spin and crashed with no survivors.

The Plane of a Thousand Flights

This is a good design for stunts, but it can
fly straight ahead as well!

1. Fold the paper in half the long way. With
   a ruler, find and mark the center point of
   that fold.

2. Make a horizontal fold across the bottom,
   bringing the bottom middle up to your
   mark.

3. Fold in each corner perfectly.

4. Then fold each side of the paper up to make a V shape.

5. Fold the whole thing in half. Now fold the wings just like you did for the glider: fold the wings on each side by folding from the point to the end and making the top align with the bottom.

6. Unfold the wings so they are flat.

This plane really flies differently with different modifications. If you tape the body tight on top and give it elevators folded up, it will fly well straight ahead. If you curl the back outside edges of the wings and throw the plane somewhat upwards, it can boomerang. If you hold the wings away from you and throw it with the nose straight up, it can loop de loop. Experiment away!

Helicopters

The rotors on a helicopter are basically spinning wings. By spinning, they create lift for the machine, and if you tilt the spinning mechanism slightly, the helicopter can move in any direction. More importantly, a helicopter can hover!

Quick Copter

If you have some paper, two straws, Scotch tape, and some Playdoh or clay, you can crank out a copter!

1. Cut 2 pieces of paper that are 2½ inches across and 4 inches long.

2. Tape one straw to the other to form a T shape. Put a little lump of clay at the bottom of the T.

3. Gently fold the pieces of paper over the ends of the "arms" of the straw T. Tape the other side of the paper to hold it together,

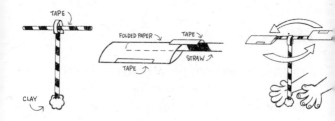

and put a little tape between the paper and straw to keep it in place. Look at the diagram for how to do this properly.

4. Holding the vertical straw, slide or brush your hands together to create lift. The Quick Copter will rise up and away!

No-Rotor Helicoptering Hovercraft

What makes helicopters unique is their ability to hover. Here's a futuristic design that eliminates the rotors!

YOU NEED: glue; an empty thread spool; a CD you don't want anymore; a button; a balloon

1. Glue the spool to the old CD so that the holes in the middle line up.

2. Let it dry and then glue the button to the top of the spool. (The holes should still line up!)

3. Now blow up the balloon and stretch its mouth over the top of the spool/button. (Don't let the air escape while you do this.)

4. Set the contraption on a smooth surface and let go of the balloon. The device will float along and hover over the table as it scoots!

Rockets

Many people will describe someone who is smart as a *rocket scientist.* This is weird, because a rocket is the simplest kind of engine there is. A car engine is much more complicated. From now on, if you want to say someone is smart, say that they are a real *auto mechanic.* It makes more sense!

You can become a rocket scientist pretty easily. First, let's look at how a basic rocket works. Rockets are powered with some kind of *force* that propels them upward. This force may be a liquid fuel that burns and turns into a gas, like kerosene. Some rockets use a solid fuel instead, like many fireworks do. Rockets can even use only air or water for their propellant! (For detailed plans on how to make impressive air and water rockets, see the book *Backyard Ballistics* by William Gurstelle.)

★*GRAVITY STUNTS YOUR GROWTH!* Rocket-riding astronauts grow from 1½ to 2½ inches while in outer space. Without gravity pulling them down, they get taller! (Hey, what do you have if you tangle your shoelaces in outer space? *Astro-knots!* Okay, sorry.)

Rocket Basics:

★ HAVE PARENT SUPERVISION FOR ANY ROCKET EXPERIMENT.

★ LAUNCH YOUR ROCKET IN AN OPEN AREA AWAY FROM AS MANY ROADS, TREES, AND ROOFS AS POSSIBLE. (YOU SHOULD ALSO TAKE THE WIND INTO ACCOUNT.)

★ WEAR PROTECTIVE EYEWEAR IN CASE OF A BLOWUP ON THE LAUNCHPAD.

★ FOLLOW DIRECTIONS, AND DON'T CHANGE OR SKIP STEPS!

★ FINALLY, USE YOUR COMMON SENSE! FOR EXAMPLE, DON'T EVER PUT SOMETHING (LIKE YOUR FACE) OVER THE ROCKET ONCE IT IS STAGED FOR A LIFTOFF.

Model Rockets

Model rockets are also sometimes called "solid fuel rockets." Solid fuel rockets have a charge (or "grain") that burns smoothly once it's ignited. These rockets come in kits (found in any hobby shop or toy store) that supply the motor and the rocket. You can usually use the rocket again, but you have to buy more motors sooner or later. Although they can be expensive, model rockets are a blast.

Okay, it's not a model rocket, but here are the plans for making the world's cheapest and easiest solid-fuel rocket.

Match Rocket!

It was a great day when I learned that with a match, I could make a rocket that really zips. Some people get theirs to go as far as 50 feet!

YOU NEED: Cardboard; matches; foil; two

126

needles (pins will work if you don't have them)

1. Do this outside with adult supervision in a place where a fire can't start.

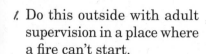

2. Cut a piece of foil 1-inch square.

3. Tear out a match. (Wooden matches can also work, but I like cardboard ones.) Make a straight cut at its end where it was connected to the matchbook.

4. Lay the match near the edge of the foil. Half of the match should be sticking off the foil.

5. (Optional) Now cut the head off of another match and lay it at the end of the head already in the foil.

5. Put the needles on each side of the match, with the sharp ends near the match head.

6. Leaving a "pointy head" on the assembly, carefully roll the foil around the match and pins. Make sure to *completely* close the foil and get it as *tight* as possible around the match. Do a good job wrapping the needles! You should end up with an aerodynamic shape.

7. Pull the needles out, leaving two small holes on each side of the match. (Be careful not to crush these holes shut, or it won't work!)

8. If you have a launcher that you want to use, put the rocket in it, with the holes facing down. (I use a hollowed out pen, but any piece of hard plastic or metal tubing will do. Keep one end of your launcher blocked off.) You can also just set the rocket on an incline with the head protruding and it might take off.

9. Stand to the side of the rocket and hold a flame on the foil. A lighter actually works better than a match for this. Try to move the flame around a bit so you don't burn a hole in the foil; you just want to heat up the assembly enough to ignite the match heads!

10. Watch the Match Rocket fly away!

PROBLEMS? Make sure you're wrapping that foil as tight as you can. Try adding another match head to the mix. Try using one needle instead of two. Wrap a little tape around the foil to prevent blowouts. Or, if you have another kind of foil, use that to wrap the match. Still no good? Write me at *kingbart@comcast.net*.

Air ("Pneumatic") Rockets

Just like a blowgun shooter uses a puff of air to shoot the dart, air rockets rely on a fast jet of air to get liftoff. This kind of force is called a "pneumatic" (new-MAT-ic) force.

Chapstick® Lip Balm Rocket

Here is how to make the world's simplest air rocket: The Lip Balm Rocket, made by using a Chapstick® brand lip balm tube! When your chapped lips have used up all the balm in the container, follow these steps for a hand rocket that can be fired at will!

YOU NEED: an empty lip balm container

1. Remove the cap of the container. Save it.

2. Remove the end of the container by using a penny to pop the turning device off the bottom of the tube, which includes the plastic threaded dowel. (This has to be pulled out of the part that contains the balm.) Save it.

3. Remove the cup that holds the balm. Dig out any balm still in there.

4. Reverse the cup so that the hollowed portion faces the bottom of the tube and

130

stick it back where it came from. Push it all the way down to the base of the balm tube.

5. Take the threaded plastic dowel and screw it back into the hole in the plastic cup. Leave it hanging out like a plunger. This is your firing mechanism.

6. Put the cap of the container back on.

7. Hold the tube firmly. Aim the cap at something. Pull your off hand back and strike the plunger mechanism sharply with your palm.

8. The cap flies off to parts unknown!

Water Rockets

Water rockets (also called "hydro-pump" rockets) are my favorite kind of missile. Pressurized water is their fuel, and when these rockets achieve liftoff, water goes flying all over.

You're-Gonna-Get-Wet Rocket

This is a good basic water rocket for someone who likes to work on a project!

YOU NEED: scissors; thin cardboard; duct tape; a plastic soda bottle; a couple of feet of plastic tube (aquarium shops have this); an air valve (the pointy thing you shove in a ball when you blow it up with air); a cork that will fit in the neck of the bottle; an awl or ice pick to drill a hole through the cork; a bicycle pump

1. Cut out 3 or 4 fins from the cardboard in the general shape shown; make them between 7 and 9 inches long.

2. Duct tape the fins to the bottle (with the fins at even

132

distances) so the bottle can stand up on its own.

3. Take your tube and fit the air valve into one end of it. Have the fat end stuck in the tube and the pointy end sticking out. Now drill a hole through the cork that is just big enough to fit this end of the plastic tubing. Push the valve and tube through the cork so that the valve's pointy end comes out the end of the cork.

4. Turn over the bottle with fins taped to it and fill it about ⅓ to ½ of the way with water.

133

5. Now shove the cork into the bottle's opening! Get it in there good and tight, but not crazy tight. (It does need to be tight enough to keep water from coming out when you turn this upside down.)

6. Take the open end of your plastic tube and shove it into the tube from your bicycle pump. (If it isn't a tight fit, shove it in pretty far and duct tape the whole thing tightly.)

7. I sort of figured you were already outside, but if you weren't, take all your parts outside! Find a flat launch site away from anything that you might lose your rocket on. Turn the bottle over. Start pumping! You will see the pressure building up inside the bottle. At some point, it will be great enough to kick the cork out from its end and take off! Save all your parts and try experiments with different levels of water in the rocket.

Follow~Up Activity

Get a sheet of paper that is 20 feet across. Using one of this chapter's designs, make a giant paper plane. Get it on your home's roof, climb onboard, and have a friend give a shove. Remember to pack small bags of pretzels and peanuts for nutrition during the flight.

Gadgets, Tools, and Toys!

Here are the stories behind some of the devices that every boy should be familiar with.

Compasses

From where you are right now, there are four directions: North, South, East, and West. *You should always know where these directions are!* If you aren't sure which way is which, think about where the sun rises and sets where you live. If you are north of the equator (but not too far north!), the sun will rise in the east and set in the west. But what if the sun is directly overhead or if it's overcast?

Go get a compass. The compass is a handy tool because it will almost always point to the north. Look at your compass dial; if the needle is pointing north, then the opposite direction of north will be south! West will be to the left of north and east will be to the right.

Compasses are handy tools because of this. You know how one end of a magnet will attract another magnet, but if you reverse its end, it will repulse the other magnet? The planet Earth is a huge magnet, and the north end of the planet attracts other magnets. Your compass needle responds to this magnet and always shows you the way to the north. "Compass" north and "true" north are not quite the same thing. The magnetic north pole of the earth is actually about a thousand miles away from the "real" North Pole. This has to do with the fact that the

Earth is tilted on its axis as it rotates. The difference between true north and the compass is known as *magnetic declination,* and many maps show what the declination is.

Duct Tape

You may not have known it, but duct tape has magical powers; for example, it can get rid of warts! Army doctors have found that if duct tape is cut to fit over a wart, and then replaced once a week, the body's immune system is stimulated. This means that the wart is attacked by soldiers from the body's germ warfare system . . . *wart be gone!*

Duct tape was first made in the early 1940s to keep ammunition dry during World War II. It was originally olive green, not silver. These days, duct tape comes in all the usual colors, plus hot pink, and one brand that comes in camouflage! Since this tape is waterproof, it was first called "duck tape."

But it was so useful, soldiers were quickly using it to fix jeeps, weapons, clothing, you name it. After the war, heat experts saw that the tape was a handy thing to use on heating ducts, and the new name of "duct tape" stuck.

Although there are stronger tapes (like filament tape), duct tape, when doubled over onto itself, can pull a 2,000-pound car out of a ditch, and if they make it right, you can still rip it with your bare hands.

Frisbee

The world's earliest Frisbees may have been used for weapons. Some stories tell of how Roman soldiers over two thousand years ago fought against enemies by throwing their small, round, sharp shields at them.

ROMAN SOLDIER: *HEY, BARBARIAN! CATCH!*

BARBARIAN: *I'VE GOT IT! I'VE GOT IT! I—I—AAAIIII!"*

The next step that led to the invention of Frisbees was pies. In the 1920s, a Connecticut baker named William Russell Frisbie stamped his last name onto the tin pans in which his pies were sold. At some point, college students who had eaten the pies started throwing the pie tins through the air.

Meanwhile, a man from California came up with the idea of a plastic flying saucer. He tried to sell his saucers with names like the Pluto Platter, the Sailing Satellite, the Sputnik, and the Flying Saucer.

These sold okay in California, but not nationwide. The flying disc idea wouldn't get off the ground from coast-to-coast.

And then one day, the president of the Wham-O! toy company was at an East Coast college. He saw college students throwing around Frisbie's pie-tin lids! The students told him they called the sport "Frisbie-ing." Wham-O! took the name, misspelled it as "Frisbee," and in 1959, began releasing their new product, the flying Frisbee. A man named Ed Headrick perfected the Frisbee's design so it would fly better, and the rest is history. Ed Headrick died in 2002. He was cremated and asked that his ashes be molded into some flying discs for his family and friends. May he fly high forever!

G. I. Joe

You're a boy, and you don't play with dolls. You play with *action figures*. And if you do, you've at least heard of that granddaddy of all action figures: G. I. Joe. This soldier came out in 1964. Hasbro, the company that created him, thought about calling him Skip the Navy Frogman or Rocky the Marine Paratrooper. They finally came up with Joe's name from the World War II slang term for American soldiers: "Government Issue."

G. I. Joe was something new: A doll who came with his own flamethrower and bazooka. He was a little too warlike for some people. In 1993, a group called the Barbie Liberation Organization switched voice boxes between the talking G. I. Joe and the talking Barbie. The result was a Barbie that said things like, "Eat hot lead, Cobra!" and "Take this Jeep and get some ammo fast!" As for Joe, he got lines like, "Math is hard" and "Let's go to the mall!"

★ THE VERY FIRST G. I. JOE EVER MADE WAS PUT UP FOR AUCTION IN 2003 WITH AN OPENING BID OF MORE THAN $200,000!

★ IN A SCIENTIFIC SURVEY OF THREE BOYS AT MY SCHOOL, IT WAS AGREED THAT G. I. JOE COULD BEAT UP BARBIE'S FRIEND KEN.

★ G. I. JOE'S BICEP NOW MEASURES BIGGER THAN HIS WAIST DID IN 1964.

LEGO

These building blocks have been called "the toy of the century" and they can fascinate a boy throughout his entire life. Between the fun colors and the perfect shapes (over 1,700 of them), anybody can become an architect of the future! Heck, if you just have 6 of the 8-studded bricks, you can combine them in over a million different ways. This is why LEGO bricks are so neat: they encourage creativity.

The man who invented LEGO products was a furniture maker named Ole Kirk Christiansen. He enjoyed making wooden playthings for neighborhood children, and because he was good at this, Ole started making more money from his toys than from his "real" business. So Ole started a new business with a new name: LEGO. This word was formed by two words getting shoved together: *leg godt*. This means "play well" in Danish. (Coincidentally, it also means *"I put together"* in Latin!)

Ole Kirk Christiansen started making his building bricks in 1949, and 12 years later, they were marketed in the United

States. Today, the LEGO Company has sold so many building bricks that there are more than 50 LEGO bricks for every human on the face of the planet. And they're all lost under the couch.

PEZ

Although cigarettes are always bad for you, it is because of them that we have the wonderful invention of PEZ! Yes, it's true! A man from Austria named Eduard Haas III made a brick-shaped candy from peppermint oil and sugar. He called it "PEZ"; the letters came from the first, middle, and last letters of the German word for peppermint, *PfeffErminZ*.

Mister Haas noticed that a lot of cigarette smokers used his candy as a breath mint to help cover up their disgusting habit. This gave him the idea to make a PEZ holder shaped like a cigarette lighter. The first holders came out in 1948, and they made eating candy fun.

145

But the PEZ holder didn't sell well in the United States. Haas thought about the problem, and decided to put a cartoon character's head on top of the dispenser. (The first head was either Mickey Mouse or Popeye, depending on whom you talk to.) You tilted the PEZ head back and a single candy popped out. Haas also began making fruit-flavored PEZ.

These new ideas worked like a charm. PEZ added to the fruit and peppermint types some unusual choices for flavors, like flowers, menthol, vitamins, and chlorophyll.

The heads on top of the PEZ are also sometimes a little strange. The "Kooky Zoo" series had Roar the Lion, as well as a Cow, Yappy Dog, and Monkey Sailor. *(That's a kooky zoo, all right!)* The "Pals/Jobs" series had a Doctor and a Fireman (makes sense), and also the Shell Boy *(huh?)*, the Bride *(is she a pal or a job?)*, a Knight *(nice work if you can find it)*, a Maharajah, and a Pirate *(who probably is a crummy example of both a pal and a future job.)*

★ *MY ALL-TIME FAVORITE PEZ HEADS ARE COACH WHISTLE AND THE PSYCHEDELIC EYE.*

Pocketknives

What is it about a pocketknife that we like? They have a sharp blade and they fold up and fit into our pocket. They're fun to hold and to goof around with. (Of

course, pocket tools like the Leatherman Pocket Survival Tool are also cool!)

Folding pocketknives were made 2,000 years ago for Roman soldiers. These old knives had folding blades and many attachments, including a spoon and a fork. Even so, most people throughout history have preferred to carry around big knives on their belts. They were more impressive and they scared troublemakers away! It wasn't until about 400 years ago that the pocketknife got really popular (especially in America) because of its convenience for all kinds of people.

Here are some things to be aware of with your pocketknife. Whenever you are sharpening or cutting something with the blade, always move your stroke away from you! This will reduce the chances of cutting or stabbing yourself. It would be embarrassing to talk your parents into buying you a pocketknife and then have this happen.

TIMMY: *MOM, I HAVE SOMETHING TO TELL YOU.*

MOTHER: *TIMMY, I SEE THAT YOU HAVE A POCKETKNIFE STICKING OUT OF YOUR CHEST.*

TIMMY: *THAT'S WHAT I WANTED TO TELL YOU.*

Whittling

This is an easy and fun thing to do with your knife. You simply pick up a piece of wood and start cutting it down to size. Some people wear leather gloves when they whittle, so that they don't end up whittling their own hands by accident. To prevent a painful cut, make sure that the wood you pick up is not too hard and/or dead. That will make your blade stick, making an accident more likely to happen.

> Remember to carefully wipe the blade of your knife clean after cutting anything with it.

Sharpening the Knife

There are good sharpening stones available at most cutlery stores. Follow the directions that come with yours.

Putting the Knife Away

The problem with pocketknives is that it's possible to cut your finger while folding the blade into its "closed" position. To avoid this problem, make sure that all of your fingers are safely on the sides of the body of the pocketknife before folding the blade in.

Every so often, put a little oil (WD-40 works) on your blade and in the body of the knife to keep it working smoothly.

★*SWISS ARMY KNIVES* were invented in 1891 by a Swiss knife-maker named Karl Elsener. During World War II, U.S. soldiers in Europe loved his knife called the *Offiziermesser* (Officer's knife). Because *Offiziermesser* was a little hard to pronounce, the GIs just called it the Swiss Army knife, and the name stuck. Nowadays, the biggest Swiss Army knife is the "SwissChamp" model, which has 33 features, including a small spatula and a ballpoint pen.

Silly Putty

Silly Putty was invented during World War II (1939–45). The United States was in the greatest war the world has ever seen, and supplies were tight everywhere. Gas, meat, rubber, and metal all had to be rationed.

At that time, most of America's rubber came from rubber trees in Asia. Since this was not a good source anymore, the call went out for a new synthetic kind of rubber. An engineer named James Wright took on this challenge. He managed to invent a "fake" rubber that was 25 percent more bouncy than real rubber. It could stretch further, and it did not fall apart over time, it could take cold or extreme heat, and it could even lift the ink off a newspaper! It was amazing!

It was useless. Despite all its magical powers, this new rubber had no practical purpose. If it couldn't be used for a tire, the U.S. Army had no use for it. After the war, there was a large supply of this rubber that nobody really wanted.

Wright's invention was called "nutty putty," and it was mailed out to many people to see if they could find a use for the product. A toy store manager named Paul Hodgson saw some nutty putty at a party. (A nutty putty party! *Whoo-hoo!*)

Cool Trick

Shape your Silly Putty into a ball and then put the ball in the freezer for about an hour. Pull it out while it's cold and bounce it. You should notice a difference!

In 1949, Hodgson bought a big chunk of nutty putty and stuck little pieces of it into colored plastic eggs. These "Silly Putty" eggs sold like hot cakes! They sold better than hot cakes! History was made!

As for Hodgson, he became a millionaire.

Slinky

Like Silly Putty, the Slinky was invented during World War II. It was 1943 and the U.S. Navy needed help. The instruments that help a ship navigate are very delicate, and the rolling motion of the ocean can mess them up. A man named Richard James was working on a spring to help fix this problem. Richard had many springs set up on different shelves in his laboratory. One day, he accidentally knocked one of the springs off of its shelf and watched in amazement as the spring "crawled" from the shelf, to another shelf, to some books, to his desk, and to the floor!

Richard showed his discovery to his wife, Betty, and she knew immediately that it could be a great toy. She spent two days coming up with the right name for the toy: *the Slinky!*

The couple began production of Slinkys, and in 1946 they brought 400 Slinkys to a toy store. Would the strange springs made with 80 feet of wire sell? Within 90 minutes, all the Slinkys were gone. Luckily, Betty and Richard made more, and the toy is still around today. Does it have batteries? No. Do you plug it in? No. Does it have a video game that comes with it? No! And that is why I love the Slinky.

★ *THE SLINKY* is the Official State Toy of Pennsylvania. *Whoo-hoo!*

Super Ball

The Super Ball has been bouncing out of backyards and into the street since 1965. A chemist came up with the idea of squishing a rubbery substance under thousands of pounds of pressure to make it "super" bouncy, and the Wham-O! company helped perfect the recipe and get the ball into the hands of kids. The ball bounces back with 92 percent of its original force, so get out of its way unless you want a black eye! Today, everyone knows how much fun it is to pick up a bat and smash a homerun for hundreds of feet. It makes you feel like Super Boy! (Okay, okay, Super*man*. Are you happy now?)

★ IF YOU LIKE FOOTBALL, YOU HAVE TO LIKE THE SUPER BALL. BACK IN THE DAYS BEFORE THE SUPER BOWL, PROFESSIONAL FOOTBALL'S BIGGEST GAME WAS CALLED THE "WORLD CHAMPIONSHIP GAME." THE OWNER OF THE KANSAS CITY CHIEFS DIDN'T LIKE THIS NAME

MUCH. HE WAS WATCHING HIS DAUGHTER PLAY WITH A SUPER **BALL** AND HE GOT AN IDEA: THE SUPER **BOWL!**

★ IT WON'T QUITE BE A SUPER BALL, BUT IF YOU TAKE ONE RUBBER BAND AND WRAP ANOTHER ONE AROUND IT, AND THEN WRAP ANOTHER ONE . . . AND DO THIS A THOUSAND TIMES, YOU'LL HAVE A PRETTY GOOD RUBBER BAND BALL.

Gross Stuff!

The title of this chapter says it all. If you are ready to learn about disgusting, nauseating, and otherwise gross items, batten down the hatches and read on!

Barfing Department

Have you ever eaten something rotten? Or maybe you rode in the car too long, and your last meal wasn't sitting well? Your body has a solution to the problem! You can *retch, backwards bungee, vomit, make stew, hurl, blow, upchuck, heave, throw soup, feed the fish, puke,* or even *regurgitate!* But no matter what you call it, it's never any fun.

You barf when your stomach decides that a mistake has been made. Barfing is usually caused by motion sickness (boats and roller coasters are prime offenders), eating food with a lot of bacteria in it, or eating too fast and/or too much all at once. Now *everything must go!* But your body is very thoughtful. It sends you some signals before you blow chunks so that you can get ready. You get a horrible feeling that something bad is going to happen. Your mouth starts producing a lot of spit.

Don't feel bad if you puke in public. After all, an American president gave the most famous barfing performance of all time! In 1992, President George Bush Sr. was in Tokyo at an important dinner. He wasn't feeling well, and he ended up spewing into the lap of the Japanese prime minister and then falling on him. Nasty. It was all caught on television cameras, and the Japanese invented a new word in honor of the moment. *Bushuru*: To vomit in a public place.

You're in a cold sweat. And then . . . *blauuuug!*

Your stomach is a big muscle. It heaves and contracts and brings up a whole mess when you barf. Barf is full of stomach acid, which is why it leaves a rotten taste in your mouth. Be sure to brush your teeth after barfing because the acid can stain your teeth; besides, you'll feel a lot better. (The *worst feeling in the world* is when your mouth isn't all the way open

159

when you barf and some puke squirts out your nose! Aaagg!)

If your puke is ever green, congratulations. You managed to throw up something that's not from your stomach at all. Green barf has *bile* in it, and bile comes from a spot way down near your small intestine. That means you had to dig down deep for that one. Good work!

The scariest barf is called "projectile vomiting." This is what happens when a baby heaves cheesy stuff that lands on the other side of the room. Sometimes a wad of projectile vomit can go right out the window.

It is possible to vomit on purpose. By sticking a finger or other small item (like a feather) down the throat, a person can gag and vomit. Why would someone do this? In ancient Rome, the custom was to have huge feasts with many different kinds of food. If a person wanted to continue eating but was too full to do so, he visited the Vomitorium. This was an area to barf, where servants would clean up the mess. A philosopher from that time named Seneca once wrote that the Romans *"vomit so that they may eat and eat so that they may vomit."*

To avoid barfing, try pushing down on your wrist an inch or two up from your palm. (There are wristbands that do this for you.) This works well for motion sickness. A sip of ginger ale can mellow out your stomach, as can a saltine cracker if you're not feeling well.

There is a jet owned by NASA nicknamed the "Vomit Comet." It is used to create "zero gravity" so that astronauts can train for outer space. The aircraft climbs and dives over and over, sometimes as many as 50 times.

Funny Things to Say When Someone Barfs

"THAR SHE BLOWS!"

"ABANDON SHIP!"

"HE'S GOT THE URGE TO REGURGITATE! THROW UP ALL THAT FOOD HE ATE! VOMIT! VOMIT! YEAHHHH, VOMIT!"

Fun Barfing Facts

★ *YOU MAKE ME WANT TO PUKE!* Sea cucumbers can squirt out some or all of their guts when threatened. This is so disgusting, their would-be predator leaves. The puke is also sticky and tough. Some island cultures squirt sea cuke puke onto their feet like a pair of water shoes to protect their feet while they walk around in the water!

★ *WHEN A COW CHEWS ITS CUD*, it's basically chewing its own barf!

★*AFTER AN OWL EATS AN ENTIRE MOUSE* or other rodent, it barfs up the skin, bones, and other tough-to-digest parts in a nasty little ball called an "owl pellet." Collect them all!

Belly Button Lint, Toe Jam, and Earwax Department

Here is a strange fact to consider: You used to breathe through the hole in your stomach called your belly button. When you were in your mom's womb, all of your oxygen went through the *umbilical cord* that connected to where your belly button is now. You couldn't breathe with your lungs then; there was no air to breathe.

Now that your "cord has been cut," you use your lungs to breathe, leaving your belly button to gather dirt, dead skin, and cloth fabric. If you put all those ingredients together, you have lint! You might want to take a look in your belly button if you haven't done so lately, because it can get pretty nasty if you don't clean it out every so often.

Paramedics once responded to a 911 call for an abdominal evisceration. This means someone's guts were falling out! The paramedics went to a home and found a 13-year-old boy on a bed. When asked why he called 911, the boy said he had "stuff" coming out of his belly button. The paramedics investigated and found what the "stuff" was: belly button lint.

Lint can gather other places too. Your feet are constantly sweating, so dirt, dead skin, and cloth (from your socks) make a nice little surprise for you between your toes. We call this toe jam, although some people actually have toe jelly. Whatever you call it, don't save it up for a peanut butter sandwich. If you don't know why not, just read the "Barf" section in this chapter.

There is a place in Dawson City, in the Yukon territory of Canada, where adults can try a drink that has an actual human toe in it. It is called the Sour Toe Cocktail. The toe is a real human toe that has been preserved in alcohol and is put into drinks. As the story goes, the first toe came from the frostbitten foot of a trapper. That toe was accidentally swallowed when someone drank the cocktail too fast, and so the toe has been replaced a few times since then.

As for earwax, it is also easy to make. Just take some dead skin and mix it with the oils that are naturally in your ear. Throw in a little of the dirt that floats in your ear, and you have earwax! (I wonder why nobody ever makes candles from the stuff?) There is a woman in New England who uses earwax on her lips as a cheap alternative to lip balm, but you're probably not interested in that.

Earwax can sometimes build up to the point where it clogs the whole ear. There is nothing as surprising as innocently putting your finger in your ear and coming out with a brown chunk of gunk. Some people suffer from *ceruminosis* (see-roo-min-o-sis), or too much earwax. I once had a friend named Ben who thought he was going deaf in one ear. The doctor stuck a small metal instrument in his ear and pulled out an orange cork that had plugged up his hearing hole. He could hear again! The first thing he heard was the doctor saying, "That is disgusting."

Ben got off easy, though. Cockroaches like to find small, dark, greasy hiding places to hide out in. Guess where they some-times go? *"Nooooooooo!"*

Burping and Belching Department

Burping and belching are the same thing. You know how to burp, right? Heck, you've been doing it ever since you were born; you would swallow down air while sucking on your bottle, and then your parents would burp you. Why is belching so cool? Because everyone does it and it makes a fun noise.

In some cultures, a good belch after a meal is a sign of good manners. Of course, you don't live in one of those cultures, but never mind that.

Tips on Belching

Belching is simply a way of relieving excess gas in your stomach through the mouth. Some people can belch on command; these people have a belching super-power! However, most of us need a little help to belch. Fizzy drinks are always a good source for that extra gas.

Get a fizzy drink. *Do not shake it!* This will cause the can or bottle to burp on you when it opens! Instead, open it normally. If you have a straw, use it. Straws put more air in your system. Or just slowly drink a

The BURPING OLYMPICS

few mouthfuls, swirling the drink around in your mouth before swallowing. When you've built up enough gas, let 'er rip!

One good thing to have when you burp is gravity. This allows only the air to come up from your stomach. Astronauts in outer space have learned to try and never burp: if they do, there's a good chance that EVERYTHING in the stomach will come up at once.

There are many different things that one can do with a burp. Try some of the special belch varieties below.

VOLUME: How loud can you belch? Can you scare the dog? Can you make your grandmother's wig jump off her head?

GROSSNESS: Can you make it sound wet?

LENGTH: How *lonnnng* can you burp? Keep going till you run out of breath.

TRICKS: Can you say something while you are burping? Try saying a funny phrase; it will be that much funnier if you're belching when you say it! How about a belch that sounds really low or high? Try saying the "ABCs" with one burp!

WARNING: DO NOT DO THIS IN FRONT OF VISITING RELATIVES, IMPORTANT VISITORS, OR THE PRESIDENT OF THE UNITED STATES. ALSO, NEVER TRY TOO HARD TO BURP! YOU MAY BRING UP SOMETHING BESIDES GAS. (SEE THE "BARFING DEPARTMENT.")

And remember . . . Always say, "Please pardon me," after a good belch!

Fun Belching Facts

★*A GOOD BELCH* can escape your body at 50 miles per hour!

★*IF YOU WOULD LIKE TO* use a fancy word for belching, try "eructation." (ee-ruk-tay-shun)

★*PEOPLE BELCH,* even when they are asleep! "*Zzzzzz . . . buuurrrrpp!*"

★*BACK OFF, MONKEY BOY!* Orangutans use loud belches to warn intruders away from their territory.

B.O. (Body Odor) and Sweat Department

I've got some bad news for you: Men sweat about 40 percent more than women. Heck, your feet alone sweat out ¼ cup of sweat a day. Dang it, you are *disgusting!* If you don't sweat much now, don't worry. You will. Once you become a teenager, you'll be a sweaty beast with reeking pit stains. The good news is that sweat doesn't stink. Hurray! The bad news is that bacteria that grow in your sweat do stink.

Germs called bacteria live all over the outside and inside of your body. As soon as you sweat, bacteria start swarming all over your skin. Then you reek! But remember, it is not your fault.

The skin of your face has about two million bacteria on it. That's actually pretty good compared to your armpits. The skin on your pits is home to 516,000 bacteria per square inch. But both your face and your armpits have to take the backseat to your mouth. More than 10 billion creatures live in there. Can you taste them? They can taste you! If you have bad breath, they are the reason why. Now go buy some mouthwash.

You may bathe or shower every day, but different cultures have different ways of looking at bathing, body odor, and bacteria. In France, over 50 percent of the people *don't* bathe every day, 50 percent of the men *don't* use deodorant daily, and 40 percent of the men *don't* change their underwear daily. You add up all those *"don'ts"* and someone smells like *"doo-doo."*

★*IT IS POSSIBLE* to give off three gallons of sweat on a hot day.

★*IN OUTER SPACE*, your B.O. doesn't leave your body; it surrounds you in a tight, stinky cloud!

Bombing Department

Some people call this tooting or farting. In this book, I will call it *bombing*. This is what happens when gas comes out your back end: you drop a bomb! Sometimes it is noisy and sometimes it is quiet, but it's

usually stinky. Bombs are like belches; they are funny because they make a weird sound and everybody does it. And I mean everybody. Benjamin Franklin, founding father of the United States, even wrote a book called *Fart Proudly!*

So where do your bombs come from? Part of a bomb comes from swallowing air while you suck on candy, chew gum, and eat. People who gulp their food usually bomb more than those who don't. But your body also makes gas naturally. As you digest food, gases are created in your intestines and will exit your back end faster than 30 miles per hour.

How big, long, and stinky your bomb will be depends on how long you've been holding it in and what you've been eating. Another factor is what kind of *bacteria* you have in your intestines. The bacteria are what give your bombs a gas called *methane*. (Methane is an important gas because it can catch on fire!) Bacteria bombs with a lot of methane tend to be hot, stinky, and silent! A bacteria bomb is known as an "SBD"—*"Silent But Deadly."*

The most embarrassing thing known to mankind is to bomb and have the whole world know it was you. Long ago, a gentleman was in the court of Queen Elizabeth I (1533–1603) of England. He bowed to her and accidentally bombed loudly. Everyone heard! The man was so humiliated, he traveled away from England for seven years before returning to the queen's court. Once he returned, Queen Elizabeth smiled and said, "My Lord, I had forgot the fart."

Tips on Bombing

If you want to bomb, enjoy a helping of raisins, corn, white bread, cheese, bell peppers, turkey, onions, broccoli, cabbage, or brussels sprouts. Then sit back, relax, and watch the sparks fly. *Want loud bombs?* Eat some beans! You know what they say: beans on Saturday, bubble bath on Sunday. *Want stinky bombs?* Eat prunes, bran, cauliflower, or a lot of meat. Hard-boiled eggs are good for these bombs because an egg yolk contains sulphur, which is what creates the terrible smell of rotten eggs.

175

GOOD NEWS: Farts usually break up pretty quickly, so if nobody has smelled yours within a few seconds, you've gotten away with it. (This is *not* true if you are in a small space like an elevator, a classroom, or Rhode Island.)

BAD NEWS: Your nose will never be more sensitive to bad smells than when you are about ten years old. So if you're in a small space like an elevator, a classroom, or Rhode Island, breathe through your mouth just in case.

HOW TO AVOID BLAME: Okay, you feel a bomb coming on and you're in a public place. What to do? If you're seated, don't innocently lean over to the side to let it out. Take it from me, this has never fooled anybody. Way back in 1530, a man named Erasmus wrote, *"Do not move back and forth in your chair. Whoever does so looks like he is trying to bomb!"* (That's almost an exact quote.)

Remember

Politeness is important, so try to avoid bombing in public if possible. Say, *"Please pardon me,"* if you do bomb in public. You're lucky to have that right; in China 2,500 years ago, it was illegal to bomb in front of other people. Finally, never try too hard to push a bomb out. You might be *very, very sorry.* You've heard the old expression, "Where there's smoke, there's fire?" Well, where there's a bomb, there's poop! Your body can tell the difference between poop and gas, but it has trouble with liquid. So if you have diarrhea, sit on the toilet every time you think you have to bomb.

Let's say you're at school and you accidentally drop a bomb in class. Try coughing or dropping a book to cover up the sound. If you can't do that, *blame the dog!* Oh wait, the dog's not in your class! Oh well, you will have to act innocent. If you have a friend nearby, give him an accusing glance to suggest he did it. If anyone accuses *you* of bombing, remember the classic comeback line: *"He who smelt it, dealt it!"* Or, if there is no denying that it was you who bombed, just smile and wave at the people around you and say, "Just trying to make you feel at home!"

The Most Amazing Act in the World

Joseph Pujol (1857–1945) was a French stage performer whose nickname was "Le Pétomane"—*The Fartomaniac*. As a child, Joseph was told that he must avoid swimming. The problem was that the water would go into Joseph's back end, and he would begin to sink! Joseph soon found that he had the rare ability to bring air in through his rear end. He could then let the air back out and make sounds while doing so. In other words, he could make butt bongos any time he wanted to, and they didn't smell! Joseph could bomb in many different sounds and for incredible lengths of time. Some of his imitations included cannons, thunder, all types of

Other Terms for Bombs

FLATULENCE

BACKDOOR TRUMPETS

AIR BISCUITS

MORNING THUNDER

CUTTING THE CHEESE

BARKING SPIDERS

DEPTH CHARGES

BUTT BONGOS

WIND BENEATH YOUR WINGS

LAYING AN EGG

STINK-TAIL

dogs, different birds (including ducks and owls), bees, frogs, and pigs. As a show closer, Le Pétomane would blow out a candle. He almost always got standing ovations, and during his peak, he earned more money per performance than any other entertainer in Paris.

Fun Bombing Facts

★*BOYS AND GIRLS BOMB THE SAME AMOUNT,* but girls hold them in more to be polite, so their bombs are probably bigger.

★*MOST PEOPLE BOMB ABOUT 14 TIMES A DAY.* (This is about enough to fill a liter soda bottle.) If you bomb more than this, you have a super-power!

★*THE DOG DID IT!* If your dog has bad gas, you aren't feeding it the right kind of food; its intestines can't digest the food properly, creating gas.

★*THE BEAVER DID IT!* Native Alaskans enjoy a delicious dish called "stinky tail." It's not what you think; it is fermented beaver tail, which is made by burying the beaver tail in a pit for weeks or even months.

★*THE ELEPHANT DID IT!* Elephants do drop huge bombs, but luckily they don't smell too bad. The *worst smelling* bomber in the animal kingdom (besides your dad) might be the turtle. The *loudest* bomber in the animal kingdom is the donkey. But the animal that bombs the *most* is the termite! Their bombing is actually causing global warming. (Hey, if you ate wood, you might have some digestive problems too.)

Creatures Department

There are some gross animals out there and the leech is definitely one of them. Leeches are relatives of earthworms; they live in very wet environments and they want to suck your blood. Leeches range in size from tiny to more than 2 feet. Leeches may clamp onto your legs, but they also like to swim to a dark crevice where you won't find them, like your armpit, your butt, or worse! (No, I did not make that up. Luckily, these types of leeches are usually only found in Africa, Asia, and islands in the Pacific and Indian oceans.)

Leech "bites" are painless, so you probably wouldn't notice if a leech has attached itself to you. If you find a leech on you, don't cut it off. You could cut it in half, and it would keep sucking. In the movies, adventurers often put the lit end of a cigarette on the leech to make it let go, but since you don't smoke, this won't work. Instead, put salt, lemon (or lime) juice, or an ice cube on the leech. Then it will let go.

Inside of you may be another foul creature. Tapeworms anchor themselves deep in the guts of animals (like you!). They then hang out, eating the food that is passing through you. Don't worry, though, they don't get very big . . . just up to 100 feet long or so! (See, your guts go around and around inside of you . . . and so does the tapeworm!)

Probably the most disgusting creature in the water is the lamprey. This is a fish that looks like a combination of an eel and your worst nightmare. Baby lampreys live under mud and ooze out mucus and phlegm that traps victims long enough to be eaten. When baby lampreys are big enough, they swim after their food. They have a mouth that is round and a tongue that will saw through the skin of its victim. See, when a lamprey sees another fish that looks like good suckin', it attaches itself to the fish and sucks out all of its life-juice. That's right, lampreys suck.

As gross as the lamprey is, it's not much worse than the slime eel, or "hagfish." This delightful denizen of the deep is covered in mucus, which discourages other fish from coming near it. The slime eel is made up entirely of intestine; it has no stomach. It swims along the bottom of the sea floor and looks for fish that are either dead or sick. The slime eel then goes in the fish's mouth or gill or eye and eats it up from the inside out, using its tooth-covered tongue to scrape the food to bits. *Blech!*

★*THE AUSTRALIAN SOCIAL SPIDER FEMALE* gives birth to many babies at once. Unlike other spiders, the Australian Social Spider then lets her babies suck her juices out. The little brats then puke all over her and eat the dissolved mess. *Yum.*

★*KIWI BIRDS* are small black birds found only in New Zealand. Kiwis lay some of the biggest eggs in the bird world: a five-pound kiwi can lay a one-pound egg! That's sort of like a 90-pound boy busting a grumpy that weighs 18 pounds!

★*A SPANISH VISITOR ONCE SAW* a number of bags in the palace of Montezuma, the ruler of the Aztecs (an ancient American people). The visitor thought the bags were full of treasure, and opened them up. The bags were full of squirming lice! The Aztec people believed that even if they were broke, they could still show respect to Montezuma by picking lice off their bodies and giving the creatures to him.

Dandruff and Hair Department

Dead skin is falling off of you all the time. About 80 percent of the dust in your house comes from dead skin cells. If we added up all of your dead skin and dandruff, more than ½ pound of it falls off of you in a year. Try saving yours up and then using it for confetti at a party!

Bald people are lucky. Not only are they more intelligent than most people, but we (oops, I mean *"they"*) usually don't have the dandruff problems that people with hair do. That's because hair keeps dead skin cells from falling away from the body. Instead, the dead cells get clustered together and break off in bigger chunks of dandruff, or *"seborrheic scruff,"* as the doctors call it. Hurray for bald people!

People have been shampooing, dying, clipping, and shaving their hair ever since humans have been around. It seems silly to spend so much time on it. Three out of five American women color their hair, but men can be just as foolish. In ancient Rome, men combed earthworm paste into their hair to keep from going gray. (They also rubbed bear grease on their heads to keep from going bald!)

★*HEY, FAT HEAD!* In your room are tiny dust mites that eat your dandruff. But your dandruff is so high in fat that the mites have to wait for a fungus to lower the fat content before they chow down. *"Mmmm . . . dandruff!"*

Food Department

I can remember coming into the kitchen one morning and seeing my mom frying something up in a pan. It looked like scrambled eggs, but it was sort of *blue*.

"WHAT IS THAT?" I ASKED.

"SCRAMBLED CALF BRAINS," MY MOM ANSWERED. "WANT SOME?"

Yech! My mom also liked to make *head-cheese*. To make this, she would take a pig's head, remove all of its meat (you know, the lips, eyes, tongue, cheeks, snout, etc.), wrap it in a cloth, boil it, stick it in the refrigerator, and leave it there. When she came back to it later, a clear gelatin had magically formed over the whole mess. She would then stick the headcheese on a cracker and eat it with a smile. Not good!

Different cultures enjoy different foods. In the American Southwest there is a low-fat meat that tastes a lot like crab called "rattlesnake meat." Over 60 million guinea pigs get fried up in Peru each year, and they eat cats there too. (They say it tastes like rabbit.) But eating cat might be preferable to some Chinese foods like worm soup or sun-dried maggots.

I think you can see where I'm going with this: foods can be scary or ugly or disgusting. One of the scariest foods on the planet might be a snack that natives of the Amazon Basin sometimes enjoy: tarantula! Tarantulas can be barbecued or roasted on the coals of a fire in a large leaf. Those in the know say it tastes like shrimp, not chicken.

There are many ugly *sounding* foods. For example, there is a cold Polish soup called "Chlodnik" (*"Another bowl of delicious Chlodnik, dear?"*). Other favorites of mine are "bladder wrack" (an edible seaweed), "bloater" (a dried fish), "Skum Saus" (a scummy sauce from Norway), and "Brat-klops" (German fried meatballs). But it is hard to beat *"Wiener Krapfen"* for a bad name. Is it a combination of wieners and, uh, you know? Nope, it's a doughnut in Austria.

One of the *ugliest-looking* foods in the world might be a fungus called *smuts*. Smuts is a parasite that grows on corn or other grains. It looks like a sooty, gray tumor. Some say that it also *tastes* like a sooty, gray tumor. Another dish that isn't very pretty is an Icelandic meal called "Svid." To make Svid, cut off a lamb's head. Boil it. Eat it. You don't mind your meal looking back at you, right?

But for the world's most *disgusting* food, our judges have narrowed it down to five contestants. Coming in fourth place is a Vietnamese food called "Nuoc Mam." It is made by burying fish in salt until they digest themselves with their own stomach acid and then turn into fish sauce. Yummy!

In a tie for third place, we have two similar recipes. From Iceland is a dish called "Hakarl." To make it, take a shark and remove its guts. Then hide the shark in a wooden barrel for 3 years. When you come back, it should feel like cheese and smell like, well, like a fish that you left in a barrel for 3 years. Now eat it! Another crowd-pleaser from China is called "Pi-tan." Soak some chicken eggs in a liquid made of tea leaves, lye, and a couple of other ingredients for about three months. Then bury them for 4 years. After you've built up your appetite for that long, dig the eggs up, peel them, note the green yolks and delicious odor, and swallow 'em down!

Coming in second place is a French meal called *Yeux de Veau Farcis*. You may have noticed that cows have fairly big eyes. Well, for this recipe, you'll need two of them. Boil the cow eyes for a minute, cut out any part that isn't white, and stuff them with mushrooms. Now you're ready to fry up a couple of eyeballs!

In first place (drum roll, please) it is the Scottish New Year's recipe for *haggis*. Get a sheep's stomach and fill it with oatmeal, fat, and a sheep's cut-up liver, heart, and lungs. Let it simmer for four hours, and then pour Scotch whiskey over the whole thing. (If you're smart, you'll then set the whole mess on fire.)

The poet Robert Burns described haggis as "gushing entrails" (and he was trying to be nice!). Scots usually eat haggis with "neeps and tatties"—mashed turnips and potatoes. Once, a shipment of haggis was not allowed into the United States because it was considered "unfit" for humans to eat.

★ *READ MY LIPS: I DON'T WANT ANY!* Once upon a time in Vietnam, orangutan lips were considered a delicious snack.

★ *YOU KNOW THAT WAXY SMELL THAT YOU GET WHEN YOU OPEN A BOX OF CRAYONS?* That smell is *beef fat*. Processed beef fat (called *stearic acid*) is an ingredient in many crayons. A study found crayons to be the 18th most recognized odor in the nation; as for the taste, crayons are somewhere between wax, soap, and beef fat.

Pee Department

If you are average, you pee about 1 to 2 quarts of urine a day. Did you know that all of that fresh pee you're making is actually "cleaner" than your spit? That's because no bacteria can live in pee. And to think that you *swallow* spit . . . hmmm. Actually, because fresh pee is mostly water (with some salt and unneeded proteins) it is so clean, you *can* drink it. (I'm not saying you *should* drink it.) Believe it or not, you have drunk pee before. We all drink pee before we are born because the fluid we float in contains our own baby pee! The famous world leader Mahatma Gandhi drank a bit of pee each morning to get his day off to a p-p-perfect start.

An interesting thing about pee is that it has no odor. Even if you take vitamins and eat asparagus, your pee won't stink until it begins to break down. Of course, as soon as your pee hits the air, it breaks down, so that's why it can be smelly when you're pretending to be a firefighter.

A sensitive subject for many boys is bed-wetting. Don't feel bad if this has been a problem for you. One out of every 7 kids is a bed-wetter! (One percent of all 18-year-old boys still wet the bed.) If you are worried about bed-wetting, try eating some crackers or having a spoonful of honey before going to bed. Either of these items will help you retain your water. (In ancient Rome, they used to make bed-wetters eat boiled mice, so we've come a long way!)

ONE LAST THING: Your pee is also as warm as you are when it comes out. This means that whenever you are in the cold weather, you should try to write your name in the snow in big yellow letters!

★*LOVE IS A PRICKLY THING!* Male porcupines look for their mates in the autumn. When the male porcupine sees a female, he sprays her with pee to see if she's interested in him. If she stays, she likes him. Now that's love!

193

Useful Advice

You're in class and really need to pee, but you don't want to say, "I need to go to the baffroom" in front of other students. Instead, raise your hand and say, "I need to micturate." All teachers know that this means you have to go pee, and will give you a hall pass!

Important Warning

If your pee is a dark brownish-yellow color, you need to drink more water. Your body needs lots of clear fluids to flush itself out properly, and soda doesn't cut it.

A More Important Warning

Never pee on an electric fence! You see, water conducts electricity, and . . . oh, it's just too awful to think about.

Colorful Sayings

"FULL OF PEE AND VINEGAR": THIS MEANS "FULL OF LIFE."

"GO PEE IN YOUR HAT" OR "GO PISS UP A ROPE": THESE MEAN "GET LOST."

"PEE INTO THE WIND": THIS IS USED TO DESCRIBE ANYTHING FOOLISH OR FUTILE.

"IT'S A PISSER": THIS MEANS "IT'S AMAZING."

"PISSING AND MOANING": THIS MEANS "COMPLAINING."

Fun Pee Facts

★*AVERAGE PEE TIMES*—girls: 80 seconds; boys: 45 seconds. Wee-wee win!

★*BIRDS DON'T PEE AT ALL.* Their pee mixes with their poop, sometimes turning it white.

★*ANCIENT ROMANS* brushed their teeth with pee and also used it as mouthwash. They thought pee kept teeth firm in their sockets and white. (Talk about "potty-mouth"!)

★ *THAT'S WHAT I CALL "HOLDING IT!"* When bears hibernate during the winter, they never get up to go pee in the woods. Their body simply reuses the fluids.

★ *THAT'S WHAT I CALL "HOLDING IT" TOO LONG!* Tycho Brahe (1546–1601) was a famous astronomer from Denmark who was very polite. It was customary to not get up from the dinner table to pee until the meal was finished. Some people believe that Tycho "held it" too long at the dinner table one night, and his bladder burst. Brahe apparently died of pee poisoning (aka, "septic shock") days later.

Poop Department

Did you know that some of your strongest muscles are deep *inside* your body? These muscles are there to keep your digested food moving along. That's right, you have a Playdoh Fun Factory inside of you! The muscles squeeze in a wave-like motion called *peristalsis* (pear-ih-STALL-sis), so that poop is always moving through your system.

After your digestive system has taken the vitamins and water from your food, what's left over is what scientists call "poop." About ⅓ of the food you eat becomes poop. This includes a lot of vegetable and grain fibers. Most of the rest of it is bacteria. (Up to ¼ of your poop can be bacteria!) It eats at the poop as it goes through your intestines, and the bacteria leaves behind chemicals that make your poop stink. The more bacteria in your poop, the more it stinks. Add some "bile" from your gall bladder, which helps break down fats and gives your poop a nice brownish-green color, and you're ready for a very special delivery.

But your special delivery may never arrive if there is not enough water in your body. If you are dehydrated, your poop will dry out and slow down in your guts. (Some people call this a *plugged drain,* a *logjam,* or *clogged plumbing.*) It's like dry plaster is inside of you; it will move slowly, and when it comes out, it will be hard and painful. If your poop doesn't come out, try jumping up and down, eating some prunes, and drinking a lot of water to break up that plaster!

Poop Tales!

Diarrhea caused one of the best scenes in the film *Indiana Jones and the Raiders of the Lost Ark.* In one part of the film, Indiana Jones is attacked by a swordsman who is doing amazing tricks. Indie just pulls out his gun and shoots him. This scene was supposed to be much longer and would have taken three days to film, but actor Harrison Ford *really* had to go. (He had picked up a bad case of diarrhea on location.) Ford and director Steven Spielberg came up with this much shorter solution to the swordsman scene.

If the food you ate is not agreeing with you, something weird happens: your body tries to get it *out* of you as soon as possible! Instead of water being taken *from* the poop, water is *added* to it to make it run through your guts fast, like water through a pipe. When it comes out the other end, we call it DIARRHEA!

Funny Things to Say While Pooping

"LOOK OUT BELOW!"

"CAPTAIN, WE HAVE A MESSAGE FROM THE POOP DECK."

"GET OUT THE CHAIN SAW, 'CAUSE HERE COMES A TREE TRUNK."

"I BUSTED A GRUMPY!"

Some Categories of Poop

DIARRHEA: It can burn!

FLOATERS: They float!

SINKERS: Guess what they do?

TWO-FLUSHER: That's a big one!

WATER BREAKER: A log that starts at the bottom of the toilet, and in one unbroken piece, breaks the surface of the water.

★*HISTORICAL POOP REMOVAL!* If you are Scottish, you should feel proud. Your ancestors were the first people who could go to the bathroom indoors. Hurray! The earliest plumbing systems ever found are in Scotland. They're 10,000 years old, and yes, they still smell a bit.

★*MODERN POOP REMOVAL!* When astronauts bust a grumpy in outer space, the poop is dried and brought back to Earth for scientific analysis. The astronauts have to store it carefully; they wouldn't want to see a dried log floating around in zero gravity.

★*DISGUSTING ITEM!* Vultures enjoy eating rotting meat, but they worry about

Other terms for Poop / Pooping

NIGHT SOIL

VOODOO BUTTER

BOWEL MOVEMENT

HAZARDOUS MATERIAL

DOODY

DOO-DOO

CACA

LINCOLN LOGS

NUMBER TWO

ANSWERING NATURE'S CALL

UNHITCHING A LOAD

DROPPING KIDS OFF AT THE POOL

standing on a dead animal and getting their feet infected. To solve the problem, they poop on their own feet before perching on a corpse. Apparently vulture poop can kill even the toughest germs!

★*EVEN MORE DISGUSTING ITEM!* Eating your own poop is pretty nasty, but some animals do it; this is called "coprophagy" (kop-prof-ah-jee). Beavers have a fairly high-fiber diet, and they have to digest their food twice. Here's how it works: the beaver eats its food (tree bark) and digests it. The beaver then poops out what looks like a gelatin/oatmeal mix. What next? The beaver then eats its poop and digests it a second time. When it comes out this time, it looks like sawdust. *Sawdust!*

★*HISTORICAL POETRY!* Toilets and good sewage systems make life healthier for the people who use them. In historical times, getting rid of sewage was not always done very well, as this 600-year-old poem shows us.

In days of old, when knights were bold

And toilets had not been invented,

They laid their load by the side of the road

And went away, contented.

Scabs, Scars, and Bruises Department

You got a charley horse on your thigh and now it is turning greenish blue. It's bruise time! The bruise usually starts out purple and ends up a strange type of yellow as your body tries to deal with the injury. The problem is that you're bleeding on the *inside* of your body. What you are seeing is blood that has burst out of the blood vessels inside of you.

Maybe you actually got a cut or some "road rash" from falling off your bike. You bleed some, and then the blood clots form a scab. Once your cut has scabbed up, you may notice that it shrinks over time, causing some pinching of the skin. It's almost like your body is trying to sew the wound back together. This is also likely to cause some itching to occur, which is why people often pick at a scab.

Scab-pickers are not the lowest form of life there is, but you just know that if someone picks their scabs, they pick their nose too. It only makes sense! Anyway, sometimes a cut is so big or deep that a scab can't repair all the damage that's been done. In those cases, the body forms "connective tissue" to repair the damage. The flesh won't look the same as it was before the injury, and we call what is left a "scar."

Scurvy is a disease that sailors used to get because of a lack of vitamin C. What happens if you have scurvy? First the victim gets loose teeth, rotten gums, and joint pain. Then scabs stop healing and actually turn back into open wounds. Finally, old scars open up again; it's as if time was going backward! Old healed broken bones break again! Scurvy used to be so common among sailors, ⅓ of a ship's crew often fell victim to it as late as 1800. If you want to avoid it, suck on an orange.

Snot, Boogers, and Spitting Department

You've got a lot of *mucus* in you. The wet *mucus* in your nose traps nasty things like dust and germs from the air that you are breathing in. But what is this *mucus* made of? Well, besides the dirt that lands on it, mucus is made of water, a little salt, and a little bit of a sticky protein called *mucin*.

Mucus can dry up after it traps enough dust and dirt, and then it turns into a booger, which needs to be removed. You should know that 70 percent of people admit that they pick their boogers regularly; that means that 30 percent of people *lie about it!* If you see someone picking their nose, call them a *"rhino-tillexomaniac"* (ri-no-til-ex-o-maniac). That's fancy talk for a "nose-picker." You probably know one of these types. Heck, you probably *are* one of these types! Ever pick and flick? You know what I'm talking about!

It's not so bad that you picked your nose; it's what you do with the booger that's gross.

Out of all the nose-pickers in the world, 3 percent of them pick a winner and *eat it!* That *is* disgusting. Boogers aren't dead brain cells, so you won't get any smarter by eating them!

Now the fact is that a lot of your snot ends up going down your throat. As a matter of fact, you drink about a quart of snot a day by swallowing it. Don't worry, the acid in your stomach kills any germs that are in your mucus. In addition, your snot can lubricate your throat and help you when you need to spit. This is called *"hawking a loogie."*

As you probably know, you hawk a loogie by coughing a little bit and bringing up some of that snot in the throat. You then get it in your mouth, and *"Patooie!"* Hawk it! Loogie spitting contests are fairly disgusting, and therefore a lot of fun. Most of these contests revolve around who can spit their loogie (or "lootch") the farthest. The best you can hope for is that someone will fail to get the loogie away from themselves, and it will end up on their shirt. That always cracks me up.

I once had a neighbor who could do very well in these contests, simply by firing snot directly out of his nose. He would close one nostril with his finger and blow or snort out the other one. *Wham!* These snot rockets would fly a good distance. My neighbor called them *"Hoboken zephyrs."*

Here is a nose tip: If you have to blow your nose in front of other people, when you're done, don't look into the tissue as if precious stones fell out of your nose. They didn't. And if you thought it was a booger, it's snot.

★ *SPITTIN' FISH!* Archerfish can spit at distances over 3 feet very accurately. They spot bugs on overhanging branches from below the water, come up near the surface, and snap their gill covers shut. Wham!

★ *YOUR EYES GET DRIED MUCUS IN THEM* while you sleep. The stuff is sometimes called bed-boogers or eye-snot, but to be accurate, it is "gound."

★ *PEOPLE IN CHINA SPIT ANYWHERE THEY WANT TO.* Because of the air pollution in many of the cities, they find it best to clear the soot and gunk in their throat and nose by leaving loogies all over the place.

★*COOL WORD!* "Ambeer" is the spit juice from chewing tobacco. Come on . . .

Fun Snot Facts

★*FOR A TIME,* there was a delicious candy on the market called Snot Candy. It came in a big plastic nose. To get the gooey candy out, you had to stick a finger up the container's nostril. Of course, Snot Candy had a mascot: everyone's favorite superhero, Loogie Man!

★*THERE IS AN ESKIMO TRIBE* that has a unique solution to a baby's stuffed nose. The mother sucks the snot out of the baby's nose and then spits it on the ground!

★*WE ALL KNOW WHAT DIARRHEA IS,* but did you know you can have the same problem from your nose? "Rhinorrhea" (ri-no-ree-uh) is the word used to describe a lot of really runny mucus coming out of your nose.

Zits

Look, I'm getting a little grossed out myself. I've been writing about the most disgusting things imaginable for a whole chapter! So I'm going to write as little as possible about zits so that I don't blow chunks. Zits are little pus pockets that form on your body. During your teen years, your body starts making hormones called *"androgens"* and suddenly you have much more oil in your skin than before. The excess oil can get trapped in the sweat pores of your skin, forming whiteheads. When dirt gets trapped with the oil, blackheads appear. If these get infected with bacteria, pus is made and *ta-dah!* A zit is born!

I hate to give you bad news, but here it is: boys produce 10 times more of these hormones than girls, so boys are *10 times* more likely than girls to get really bad acne. You know that old poem that says, *"Girls are made of sugar and spice and everything nice"?* Back in the old days, this line was *"Girls are made of sugar and spice and not very much androgen."*

If you don't have zits already, get used to the idea, because the odds are that you will have at least some. What a rip-off, huh? If it makes you feel any better, eating chocolate does not make your acne any worse.

Follow-Up Activity

Interview a medical doctor for your school newspaper. Tell him that you want to invent your own internal organ and name it after yourself. Explain to the doctor what your organ does. (Hopefully, it is something disgusting.) Ask the doctor if he has any advice for you. Watch him carefully to see if he tries to call a nurse for help getting rid of you.

Riddles!

Riddle me this, Batboy: What is more fun than figuring out cool riddles? The answer: Nothing. Some of these riddles are moldy oldies that every boy should know, but *all* of them are excellent. So put on your thinking cap, Sherlock Home-Boy, and enjoy!

★*IN ANCIENT ROME,* the Saturnalia celebration was a huge party that went on for days. (The Twelve Days of Christmas would later take its place.) Riddle contests took place at that time; if you lost, you had to drink salt water combined with wine. This made you throw up. Whoo-hoo!

1. John wrote the name of a certain U.S. state on a sheet of paper in all capital letters. He then turned his page upside down and looked at it in a mirror. It read exactly as he had written it. What is the name of the state that he wrote? (*HINT:* The state doesn't start with a consonant.)

2. The 22nd and 24th presidents of the U.S. had the same mother and father but weren't brothers. How?

3. If a doctor gave you 3 pills and told you to take 1 every half hour, how long before you would be out of pills?

4. You find yourself in a bit of a pickle. You are trapped in a house that has a roomful of hungry crocodiles, a room filled with angry gorillas, and a room full of lions that haven't eaten in a year. Which room is safest for you to enter?

5. I have holes in my top and bottom, my left and right, and in the middle. Even with all of those holes, I still hold water. *WHAT AM I?*

6. Try to name 3 days that come right after one another without using the words *MONDAY, TUESDAY, WEDNESDAY, THURSDAY, FRIDAY, SATURDAY, OR SUNDAY.*

7. If a butcher is 6 feet tall, wears size 9 shoes, and has black hair, what does he weigh?

8. Look at the dollar bill. How many heads are there on both sides?

9. I'm light as a feather, yet the strongest man can't hold me for much more than a minute. *WHAT AM I?*

10. A young man and his elderly father are seriously injured in a rock climbing accident. By the time the two get to the hospital, the father is dead. An old surgeon is at the emergency room, and

when the doctor sees the injured young man, the old doctor cries out, *"THAT'S MY SON!"* The nurse replies, *"BUT DOCTOR, THE BOY WAS WITH HIS FATHER AT THE TIME OF THE ACCIDENT."* How is this possible?

11. I can turn out the lights and get into bed before the room is dark. The light switch and bed are 12 feet apart. How is this possible?

12. There are 10 white socks and 10 black socks in a drawer. How many socks must you take out (one at a time) before you are sure of having a matching pair?

13. A canoe carries only 200 pounds. How can a mother, weighing 200 pounds, and her two sons, each weighing 100 pounds, use the canoe to cross a lake?

14. In a certain season, this is a common occurrence. A man leaves home, turns left 3 times, and comes back home to see 2 masked men. Who are they? (*HINT:* It's not Halloween!)

15. There is a strange island in the South Pacific called Haircut Island. The law on this island states that you cannot cut your own hair and you must get your hair cut once a week. There are no mirrors and only 2 barbers on Haircut Island. These 2 barbers are identical twins. One barber can't cut hair very well, but his brother rules. The locals refuse to tell you which of the barbers is the good hair-cutter. You need a haircut really badly! How do you know which barber to pick for a good haircut?

16. This is a 2-part question: How many players take the field for a baseball team? How many outs in each inning?

17. Two boys have the same biological mother and father. They were born on the same day, in the same year, they look exactly alike, yet they are not twins. They are not Siamese twins and not clones, but they ARE brothers! How is this possible?

18. A sports car traveled at high speed for nearly 5 miles with a flat tire, but the driver was unaware of this. How is this possible?

19. Here is a pattern of numbers: *8 5 4 9 1 7 6 3 2* What's the next number? Why?

20. A man builds a house with 4 sides. Strangely, each side faces north. A bird goes by the house. What kind of bird is it?

21. While on safari in central Africa, Professor vanderSommen woke up and got dressed. He felt something move in the back pocket of his shorts. He reached back to see what it was. It had a head and a tail but no legs. The professor seemed unworried, and went about his chores, even after feeling the thing move in his pocket! *WHY?*

22. *I ONLY EXIST WHERE THERE IS LIGHT.*

   BUT IF LIGHT IS ON ME, I TAKE FLIGHT.

   WHAT AM I?

23. A lonely woman decided to get a pet to keep her company. She visited the local pet shop and looked around.

"WHAT ABOUT A PARROT?" the pet shop owner asked.

The woman thought this was a good idea, but as she noticed a large green parrot, she asked, *"DOES THIS PARROT TALK?"*

"THIS PARROT WILL REPEAT EVERY WORD IT HEARS. I GUARANTEE IT," replied the shopkeeper. So the woman bought the parrot.

Three weeks later, the woman still couldn't get the parrot to say a word. She took it back to the store to get a refund, but the shopkeeper wouldn't accept it back. He said his guarantee still held, though. The shopkeeper spoke the truth; how is this possible?

24. *I WAVE AND WAVE AT YOU,*

THOUGH I NEVER SAY GOODBYE.

IT'S COOL FOR YOU TO BE WITH ME,

ESPECIALLY WHEN I SAY, "HI."

WHAT AM I?

25. A donkey is tied to a 20-foot rope. A pile of alfalfa is 30 feet away. Somehow, the donkey is able to eat the alfalfa, even though the rope does not break or stretch in any way. How is this possible?

26. A woman announced that she could walk on water for 10 minutes. She said she would do it on a nearby river. A large group of people went out to watch her. They all saw her actually do it! (The river was not dry.) How was this possible?

27. An old starving wolf came upon a flock of sheep fenced in behind a tall metal fence. This fence was too high to jump over and he couldn't dig under it. The bars of the fence were close together, but because the wolf was so thin, he could just squeeze through the bars. The

problem was that if he ate any of the sheep on the other side of the fence, he wouldn't be able to squeeze back through the fence. The sheep farmer might then come and shoot him!

Puzzled, the wolf sat there. A little sheep said, *"MR. WOLF, I KNOW HOW TO SOLVE YOUR PROBLEM!"* The other sheep quickly told the lamb to keep his mouth shut! What would the lamb have said?

28. How high would you have to count before you would use the letter *"A"* in the spelling of a number?

29. A young boy who played on his school's soccer team made the following comment: *"FOUR DAYS AGO, MY SCHOOL'S SOCCER TEAM WON A GAME 4 TO 1, BUT NONE OF THE BOYS ON THE TEAM SCORED ANY GOALS. ALSO, THE OTHER TEAM DIDN'T SCORE AGAINST ITSELF ACCIDENTALLY."* How is this possible?

30. In a town in ancient Atlantis, they had a law that said all men must shave every

day. The barber in the town shaved all the men's faces, but nobody shaved the barber's face. The barber was a healthy, normal, 40-year-old person. Why wasn't the barber breaking the law?

31. Tim went to the movies with his only sister's husband's mother-in-law's only daughter-in-law. So who did he go to the movies with?

32. A man carrying three croquet balls comes to a bridge. The bridge has a sign that says, "BRIDGE CAN ONLY HOLD 200 POUNDS." The man stops and thinks. He knows that he weighs 195 pounds. Each of the croquet balls he is carrying weighs two pounds each. Assuming that this man is very well coordinated, how can he cross the bridge without having it collapse underneath him?

33. What gets wetter and wetter the more it dries?

34. A man stands in front of a painting of

a relative. The man says, *"BROTHERS AND SISTERS, I HAVE NONE. BUT THIS MAN'S FATHER IS MY FATHER'S SON."* (In other words, *"I AM AN ONLY CHILD, BUT THE FATHER OF THIS PERSON IS MY FATHER'S SON."*) Who's the picture of?

35. In heavy fog on a highway, there was a serious road crash that involved 2 trucks and 6 cars. All the vehicles were severely damaged. Police and emergency workers found both of the truck drivers and took them to the hospital. Strangely, no drivers from any of the cars could be found at the scene of the accident. Even more strangely, the police didn't seem to care! Why not?

36. *YOU THROW AWAY THE OUTSIDE AND COOK THE INSIDE.*

THEN YOU EAT THE OUTSIDE AND THROW AWAY THE INSIDE.

WHAT DID YOU EAT?

37. What is at the beginning of eternity, the

end of time, the beginning of every end, and the end of every place?

38. What is the one crime that everyone tries to prevent if they see it about to be committed, but if the crime is committed, the person is not punished?

39. I have a bow and exactly 60 arrows. If I shoot one arrow at a tree at *exactly* noon, and then shoot another arrow every minute after that, what time will it be when I run out of arrows?

40. My friend calls me up and says, "I've invented a liquid that dissolves everything it touches. Do you want to invest in my discovery?"

I say, *"MAYBE, LET ME EXAMINE IT."*

"OKAY, I'LL BRING A LITER OVER RIGHT NOW," he replies.

"NEVER MIND, I'M NOT INTERESTED ANYMORE," I tell him. Why did I lose interest?

41. A man drives his truck under an overpass, and he comes to a screeching halt. The overpass was just a little lower than the truck, and now the truck is wedged in so tightly that it can't go backward or forward. What's the easiest way to get the truck out?

42. Is it legal for a man to marry his widow's sister?

43. Is it cheaper to take 1 friend to the movies twice or 2 friends to the movies once, if you are paying for the tickets?

44. Professor vanderSommen's head lay on the desk surrounded by a pool of blood. On the floor to his right lay a handgun. There were powder burns on the right side of the professor's head, showing that he had been shot at close range. The professor's right hand still held the pen that wrote his suicide note, which was coated in blood. The police recorded the time of death as 2:00 a.m. Suddenly, the professor's best friend, Count Feely burst into the room.

"HE KILLED HIMSELF!" the Count cries. Then he sees the bloody note. *"WHY WOULD HE WANT TO KILL HIMSELF?"* he asks. You don't care about the note, because you know it was murder. How do you know?

45. What 5-letter word becomes shorter when you add 2 letters to it?

46. Look at the following pattern:

AEFHIKLMNTVWXY

BCDGJOPQRSU

Does the letter *"Z"* belong on the top row or on the bottom? Why?

47. If 3 dogs can catch 3 cats in 3 minutes, how many dogs would it take to catch 100 cats in 100 minutes?

48. While exploring the Amazon rainforest, Professor vanderSommen was seized by hostile natives. These natives told the professor that they were going to kill him

unless he could solve his way out of the following problem.

The professor had a choice of how they would kill him. Here's how it worked: The professor had to say something. It could be any sentence that wasn't a question. If the professor made a *false* statement, he would be hit with a wet noodle till dead. If he made a *true* statement, he would be forced to drink prune juice till dead.

What is the only statement that Professor vanderSommen can make which will save his life?

49. There is only one place where the U.S. flag is flying *all* day and *all* night. It is *never* taken down. It is never flown at half-mast. Where is it?

50. What is the greatest book ever written?

Answers!

1. OHIO

2. President Grover Cleveland was our only president who served two different terms at two different times (1885–1889, 1893–1897). Benjamin Harrison was the "in-between" president.

3. One hour.

4. Go in with the lions. If they haven't eaten in a year, they're dead.

5. A sponge.

6. Yesterday, today, and tomorrow.

7. Meat.

8. Fifteen: 1 George Washington head, 1 eagle head, and 13 arrowheads.

9. A breath.

10. *The doctor is the boy's mother.*

11. *I go to bed during the day.*

12. *Three.*

13. *The two sons go first. One son brings back the canoe and the mother rows over. Then the other son returns for his brother.*

14. *An umpire and a catcher.*

15. *You pick the barber with the bad haircut. The bad barber has been cutting his hair, which means he is the good haircutter!*

16. *9 and 6.*

17. *They are ⅔ of a group of triplets.*

18. *The flat tire was the spare tire.*

19. *The next number is "0." This is a listing of the numbers in alphabetical order. EIGHT, FIVE, FOUR, NINE, ONE, SEVEN, SIX, THREE, TWO, ZERO.*

20. A penguin. The only place this house could exist is on the South Pole.

21. It's a coin.

22. A shadow.

23. The parrot was deaf.

24. A fan.

25. The rope isn't tied to anything.

26. The river was frozen.

27. "Squeeze through the fence, kill one of us, tear us to pieces, and then take the pieces through to the other side of the fence. Then you can eat in peace!"

28. A thousand.

29. Girls scored the goals.

30. She was a woman.

31. His wife.

32. He juggles the balls; that way, one of the balls is always in the air!

33. A towel.

34. His own son!

35. One of the trucks was carrying a load of cars.

36. An ear of corn.

37. The letter "E."

38. Suicide.

39. 12:59.

40. If it dissolves everything, he can't bring it over. It must be a fake!

41. Let some air out of the tires and drive it on through.

42. It is both illegal and impossible, since the man would have to be dead to have a widow.

43. It's cheaper to take 2 friends once. Otherwise, you'd end up paying for 4 people instead of 3!

44. If the professor has the pen in his right hand, that means he shot himself in the head and then wrote his suicide note. Since this is not possible, it must be murder!

45. Short.

46. The letter *"Z"* belongs on the top row because it is made of straight lines, unlike the letters on the bottom, which all have a curve somewhere in them.

47. Since the 3 dogs are already averaging 1 cat a minute, you just need 3!

48. He must say, "You will kill me with a wet noodle." If the natives then kill him with a wet noodle, that would make his statement

TRUE, which means they should have made him drink prune juice. If they make him drink prune juice, this makes his statement *FALSE*, which means they should have hit him with a wet noodle!

49. The Moon.

50. You're holding it in your hands!

Slang!

One special category of words is "slang" words. These are the casual, colorful words that we like to use, like "cool," as in "This book is very cool." There are all sorts of different slang speech that you can use to make your words more inter- esting. Instead of throwing away some- thing, you can "chuck" it or "deep-six" it. Instead of jokingly threatening to beat up your friend, tell him that you will "drop him like a bag of dirt." If he gives you any back talk, tell him, "You write the check, and I'll cash it." (Nobody knows what this means, but it sounds great!)

Different countries have different slang. For example, they sure know how to speak colorfully in Australia. Here are just a few of their slang terms for "nerd" in the land Down Under: *boofhead, dag, dill, dipstick, droob, duffer, goose, and nong.*

One great source of slang is money. Money is something that everyone likes, and most people just call it "money" or "cash." But there are other great slang terms for money: *scratch, mazuma, bling-bling, shekels, dinero, greenbacks, bank, cha-ching, moolah, sawbucks, or clams.*

There are other ways to name money. Each type of paper money in the United States has a different important American on it. A good way to memorize them is to name the bill by who is on it! George Washington is on the one-dollar bill, so instead of calling a dollar a "dollar," call it a *"George Washington"* or a *"George."*

The $5 bill has Abraham Lincoln, so it can be called an "Abe." It's also sometimes called a *five-spot* or a *fiver*. Likewise, the $10 and the $20 bills can be called ten-spots and twenty-spots. I like to call the $50 bill a *"fitty."*

The $100 bill has Benjamin Franklin on it. (He was the author of *Fart Proudly!*) It's also called a *"C-note"* and a *"bill."* The U.S. Mint does not print any larger bills than that, although they used to. The biggest bill *ever* printed was the $100,000 bill. In slang, we call that *"a lot of money."*

★ *THE BUCK STOPS HERE . . . AND STAYS HERE!* When it comes to having the heaviest money in the world, the people of the Yap Islands in the Pacific Ocean take the piggy bank. There, the people use stones that can be 12 feet across and weigh more than 500 pounds! "Hey Timmy, can I borrow . . . oh, never mind."

★ *WHEN THE GREENBACK BREAKS, THE BLING-BLING WILL FALL!* Speaking of heavy money, take a crisp dollar bill. Fold it twice lengthwise so it

Special Feature: Pig Latin

Maybe you have heard someone speaking in Pig Latin before and didn't know what it was. It is an easy way to speak in a "secret" code!

Here's how it works: Any word that starts with a vowel (*A, E, I, O, U*) gets a "*–WAY*" stuck onto the end of the word. (Example: *"OWL"* becomes *"OWL-WAY."*) Words that start with a consonant (the 21 letters that aren't vowels) have their beginning moved to the end of the word, with "*–AY*" added on. It is not that hard! (Translated into Pig Latin, this becomes *"IT-WAY IS-WAY OT-NAY AT-THAY ARD-HAY!"*)

LET'S TRY SOME OTHER PHRASES:

"YOU SMELL LIKE MONKEY CHEESE" becomes *"OU-YAY ELL-SMAY IKE-LAY ONKEY-MAY EESE-CHAY!"*

"YOUR VOICE COULD PEEL SCALES OFF A DONKEY'S BUTT" becomes *"OR-YAY OICE-VAY OULD-CAY EEL-PAY ALES-SCAY OFF-WAY A-WAY ONKEY'S-DAY UTT-BAY!"*

See how great it is? Whoohoo! (*"OOHOO-WAY!"*)

looks like a "W" from the end. Rest each end of the bill on a support such as two drinking glasses. Now start putting change in the folds. You should be able to get at least $2 in quarters on it. Keep going!

Talk Like a Pirate

Being able to talk like a pirate is a valuable skill that may save your life someday. For example, let's say you were kidnapped by pirates, and they were making you walk the plank in your pajamas. You could turn to them and bellow, *"Avast, ye scurvy, chicken-livered landlubbers. If ye send me to Davey Jones' locker in these here pajamas, I'll come back and keelhaul the lot of ye!"* The bloodthirsty pirates will be so impressed, they will make you the honorary captain of the ship!

One good way to learn how to talk like a pirate is to see pirate movies, even the ones rated "Arrr!" Another way is to keep reading.

★*NOW THAT'S ONE TOUGH PIRATE:* Blackbeard (his real name was Edward Teach) was a real pirate who once shot one of his sailors without any warning. His only explanation was that if he did not kill one of his men every now and then, they would forget who he was. Blackbeard was attacked by pirate hunters in 1718. Supposedly, the corsair shouted, *"Damnation seize my soul if I give any quarter or take any from you!"* He later died of

AHOY, ME BUCKO. ARRRRRRR!

HE SAID... HELLO, MY FRIEND. IT IS NICE TO SEE YOU!

20 cutlass wounds and 5 gunshot wounds. After his death, his head was cut off, and then both head and body were thrown overboard. According to legend, Blackbeard's headless body then swam several times around the ship before sinking.

AHOY: "Hey! Hello! Yo-yo-yo!"

AVAST: "Pay attention!" or "Knock it off!" or "What the heck are you doing?"

ARRR: Good all-purpose word that can show anger, disgust, or happiness.

BILGE: "Baloney!" The *bilges* are the lowest parts of the ship that fill with *bilgewater.* They stink.

BLIMEY: "Wow!" or "Good grief!" or "Holy Toledo!"

BOOTY: Treasure or riches. If you take a bag of treasure and shake it, you are "shaking your booty."

BUCCANEER: A pirate from the Caribbean.

BUCKO: Friend. "Me bucko" is the same as "my friend."

CORSAIR: A nice word for "pirate."

CRIKEY: A good curse to use. "By crikey, I told ye lubbers to get me a fig newton!"

CUTLASS: A pirate's sword. It has a curved blade.

DAVEY JONES' LOCKER: The bottom of the sea.

DEADLIGHTS: Eyes.

DEAD MEN TELL NO TALES: A good thing to say when you're not taking prisoners. Pirates flying a red flag would kill everyone aboard any ship they fought; this was a favorite saying of theirs.

DOUBLOON: A gold coin. Doubloons are worth more than "pieces of eight."

PIECE OF EIGHT: A silver coin.

GANGWAY: "Get out of my way!" as in "Gangway, I've got to get to the poop deck!"

GROG: Usually this was watered-down rum.

(ANYTHING) HO: The word "ho" means "I see it!" The word is used for spotting ships *("Sail ho!")*, land *("Land ho!")*, and even tools *("Shovels ho!")*.

JOLLY ROGER: The pirates' skull-and-cross-bones flag. Why is Roger so jolly? Because he's about to rob you!

KEELHAUL: This was a nasty punishment. A person was tied to a rope and dragged underneath the ship. Since the sides of the ship were covered with barnacles, this would lead to nasty cuts and near-drowning.

LAD: Call anyone your age or younger this.

LANDLUBBER OR LUBBER: A person who doesn't know the sea; they "lub" the land.

LONG JOHN SILVER: One of the most famous fictional pirates, he is a one-legged character with a parrot in the book *Treasure Island* by Robert Louis Stevenson.

MAROON: Leaving a victim in a deserted area.

ME: "My."

ME HEARTIES: Good way to address a large group of people.

MATEY: A friend. *"I do not hatey me matey."*

POOP DECK: Not a place to bust a grumpy. This is the high deck at the back end of a ship.

QUARTER: Mercy. As in, *"Show me some quarter, me hearties. I really need 25 cents."*

SCURVY: This is both a disease and an insult. *Mean captain:* Why are ye movin' so slow, you scurvy dog? *Sailor:* Beg your pardon, Cap'n, but I actually do have scurvy. *Mean captain:* Oh. Sorry about that. *Sailor:* Ruff!

SHIVER ME TIMBERS: This means that you are so surprised, your timbers are shivering. The *timbers* of a ship are the lumber that the ship is made of. If they shiver, it means that you just ran into a reef, or a cannonball hit you, or the ship is just cold.

SINK ME: See "blimey."

SMARTLY: Fast or quickly. "Step smartly there, ye miserable swabs!"

SWAB: A worthless sailor who is only good for swabbing the deck.

SWAG: Booty or riches.

WALK THE PLANK: Forcing a blindfolded victim to walk along a board that extends over the ship's side. Then they drown. It apparently never was used by pirates, but that shouldn't stop us from using the cool expression!

WEIGH ANCHOR: To haul the anchor up and get ready to haul your butt somewhere else.

YO-HO-HO: This is a good all-around expression to use when singing about dead men's chests and bottles of rum.

Follow~Up Activity

Learn a foreign language. Start with the slang and "bad words" and take it from there.

Weapons!

Throughout history, weapons have mostly been used for war and violence. That's bad. Still, there are some good uses for weapons, like hunting, competitions, and self-defense.

Boys (and men) are interested in the weapons that are used for fighting. We hate the need for these deadly gadgets, but we are fascinated by them. Heck, the high point of every James Bond film is when 007 gets his high-tech weapons. Secret agents in real life have also been given some pretty strange devices. Allied

secret agents during World War II (1939–1945) who were dropped behind enemy lines sometimes carried special handkerchiefs with them. If the agent urinated on the handkerchief, a map of the territory they were in appeared!

These agents also had guns and knives hidden in unusual places. Belt buckles, gloves, mechanical pencils, and even tobacco pipes could conceal small guns. Some had a knife that was inside of a pencil. Agents were even known to carry small crossbows with them. Amazing! Speaking of *bows,* maybe we should get this chapter started with some . . .

Archery
(That's Bows and Arrows to You)

A bow is basically just a spring with string that shoots a little spear (called the arrow). What gives a bow power is that its wood is curved in one direction, but then it is strung in the opposite way. (Look at the letter C. Now imagine stringing its ends and *puulliinngg* it the other way. It would look like this: D.)

The wood used for a bow should be strong and flexible. Good sources for this wood are ash, hickory, elm, hazel, and yew. As for the bowstrings, they have been made from animal tendons, rawhide, hemp, and, of course, string.

You may hear someone say that a bow "weighs" 60 pounds. That doesn't mean that it's that *heavy;* it means that the archer needs to *pull* with 60 pounds of force to get the bowstring back. (This concept is also sometimes called "pull.") The heavier a bow weighs, the more force it shoots arrows with. The English used to use really long bows; one of them was 6 feet, 7 inches high and "weighed" 110 pounds! Longbow archers were so strong, they could kill someone with a shot from 200 yards away. Longbowmen could also shoot 10 arrows in the air; the 10th arrow was shot up before the first one came down!

There are lots of archery supplies available at sporting-goods stores and online. You may want to get (or make) a simple bow and then buy a few target arrows to see if you enjoy archery. Be sure to also get yourself an archer's glove and a bracer. These protect your fingers and forearm from the bowstring. There are also compound bows out there. Compound bows are designed so that you can shoot with great force, but because they have pulleys, you don't have to be able to pull as hard as you would with a simple bow. (Some people call this cheating.)

TO SHOOT WITH A BOW: If you're right-handed, turn so that the outside of your left shoulder lines up with the target. Hold your bow at the full length of your left arm (if you're right-handed) and notch the arrow. When you notch an arrow, don't pinch the string with your fingers. Use the "two-fingered draw." Aim from about 4 inches under your right eye; if you try to sight along the arrow itself, you'll go way too high. The farther away your target is, the higher you have to aim to make up for gravity. A bale of straw is a great target; just make sure there is nothing behind it or to the sides that could get hit!

★ *THE ENGLISH LONGBOW* was so powerful, it was known to pin a knight to his horse by going through one of the knight's legs, the horse, and the knight's other leg! (That's almost as good as the time I shot an arrow through a balloon.)

★ *THE MOST DANGEROUS FROG IN THE WORLD!* There is a frog in Central and South America about the size of your thumb. Like other amphibians, its skin gives off a toxin that discourages predators. But the golden poison arrow frog *(Phyllobates terribilis)* has a toxin so deadly that if you dip your arrowhead in it once, you'll kill anything that gets scratched with it!

Blow Guns and Peashooters

The idea of the blowgun is totally simple. If you put a small missile inside of a slightly larger pipe and then blow, your missile will come out the other end. The longer the pipe is, the more accurate your shot will be. How hard you blow and how aero-dynamic your missile is will also affect your shot. This applies whether you are using a drinking straw with a spitwad or a piece of PVC pipe and a blowdart!

TO MAKE A BLOWGUN: Get a drinking straw or hollowed-out pen. You can blow anything through it that will fit. Blow! Do NOT inhale!

What about peashooters? They are about the same size as blowguns, but you don't have to blow into them. They can really fire away, and the beauty of it is, you don't have to use peas for ammunition. Dried white beans, wood matches, spitwads, and even large, dry boogers (blech!) can be shot out of them.

TO MAKE A PEASHOOTER: It is super-easy to make. Take an empty spool of thread. If it is wooden, stick a small nail deep into the end of it. If it's plastic, Super Glue a nail or small peg to the end. This will be the end of your barrel. Now take 2 other empty spools of thread; scrape any paper off the ends of them, and then glue them together. Make sure you line them up properly so that it's a smooth line

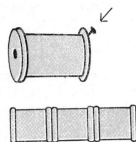

when you look down the "barrel."

To make your firing pin, you need a small stick or dowel that will fit in the barrel formed by your spools. Then take a small square of cardboard or wood, fit your firing pin into it, then glue it in place. This will prevent your firing pin from shooting out the spools along with your ammunition.

FIRING PIN

Get a good rubber band and wrap one end around the nail and the other around your firing pin block. Put your ammo in, pull your pin back, and release. Wham! It really fires hard, doesn't it? Experiment with different rubber bands and ammunition.

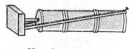

★*LIECHTENSTEIN IS A SMALL COUNTRY* between Austria and Switzerland. It used to have the world's smallest army. There was only one soldier. He served his country until

his death at age 95. Since then, Liechtenstein no longer has had an army.

BB Guns

"You'll shoot your eye out! You'll shoot your eye out!" Anyone who has seen the movie *A Christmas Story* knows the classic parent argument against BB guns: You'll shoot your eye out. My brother once shot me in the butt with his BB gun, so I can tell you something: You *could* put someone's eye out with a BB. Dang, that hurt! But (and

253

this is a big BUTT), if you are careful, BB guns can also be a lot of fun.

The first rule of any gun, whether it's a BB gun, paintball gun, or bazooka, is to assume that it is loaded. Handle the gun as if a BB (or paintball, or bullet) could come out of its barrel at any time. Because of this, you will never aim a gun at anything except your target. In addition, always keep your gun unloaded until the time when you are ready to shoot. When you are done shooting, you will completely unload the gun but still treat it as if it were loaded.

BB GUN BASICS: Before loading your BB gun, make sure the safety is on. Don't cock your gun and leave it cocked, or "dry fire" your BB gun. It isn't good for it! And I know you're not stupid, but only load a gun with its proper ammunition.

Okay, you're ready to shoot. But wait! Don't shoot yet! What if you miss? What is BEHIND or NEAR your target? Is it something that shouldn't be hit by a BB, like a glass window or your history teacher? If you are shooting with someone, you need to know where they are. BB careful!

BB guns fall under the category of air rifles. Air guns don't use gunpowder. Can you guess what they use instead? *Air!* That's right, the BB gun is basically just a fancier version of the blowgun. Some BB guns have cylinders that store air inside of them. Others have a "pump-action" that builds up air pressure. Many BB guns simply have a spring inside of them that is pulled back when the gun is cocked and released when the trigger is pulled. The spring then leaps forward and pushes the air behind the BB in the barrel, forcing it forward.

There are air guns (usually pellet guns) that have a pump on them. These types of air guns are more dangerous because the explosion of air can be made extremely strong. The Consumer Product Safety

Commission has found that there are about 4 deaths a year in the U.S. from pellet and "high velocity" (powerful) BB guns. They recommend that nobody under the age of 16 should use these guns.

★*PROBABLY THE MOST FAMOUS BB GUN WAS* the Daisy Red Ryder model, which came out in 1940. Named for a comic strip cowboy, Red Ryder had a Native American sidekick named Little Beaver. He had a cork gun named after him. It shot a cork. What a rip-off!

★ *IN ENGLAND IN THE 1800S MANY PEOPLE USED AIR RIFLES DISGUISED AS WALKING STICKS OR CANES FOR SELF-DEFENSE WEAPONS.*

Bolas

Bolas have been used since ancient times in places as far apart as Australia and Argentina. A bola is basically just a cord with weights attached to it. The bola may have 2 weights or 8, but the more weights there are, the harder it is to throw. Bolas have usually been used as a way to tangle up an animal's legs to prevent it from running away. This comes in handy when you are hunting wild prey or trying to stop Little Timmy from running off with your hat.

Try making one. For this, you will need some strong thread or heavy fishing line. You will also need 3 weights for your bola; although these weights can be almost anything, I suggest soft solid rubber balls, since they are less likely to break

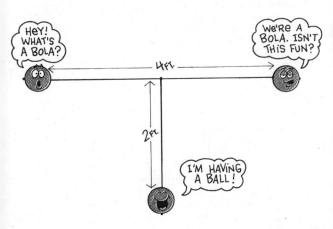

something when you are practicing your throws.

Okay, so you're using soft solid rubber balls for weights. Push a needle with your line attached through one of the balls. Once the line is on the other side, staple, glue, and/or tie it in place so that it can't pull back out of the ball. Now measure about 4 feet of the line from the other side of the ball and attach another ball the same way to that end.

Now take the third ball. Attach a 2-foot line to it and then tie the end of that line to the middle of the 4-foot line. Your bola is ready for action! Take it outside. Grab the third ball and whirl the other two around your head so that they don't get tangled. Practice on a small tree or Little Timmy and you will soon be the bola expert!

Boomerangs

Yep, boomerangs were originally weapons. However, the boomerangs we use today are used for fun, not death. You already know that boomerangs come from Australia. But do you know how they were invented? Native Australians, called "Aborigines" (aah-bo-ridge-in-eez), used a throwing stick called a "kylie" to hunt. If you missed your throw, the kylie didn't come back! At some point, an aborigine boy picked up a stick to use for a kylie and threw it through the air. The boy then turned his back on it while his friends watched in amazement. It circled around and then came back and clocked him in the back of the head! Boy, that must have been funny!

HOW TO THROW: If you have a boomerang and are ready to throw, make sure you're outside! The less windy it is, the better your throws will be. Keep away from water, trees, little kids, windows . . . you get the idea. If you make a bad throw, yell "Fore!" or "Duck!"

Okay, you're ready. Hold the boomerang vertically. Grab the boomerang wing tip in a tight grip with the curved side facing you. (One side of a boomerang is flat, and one side isn't.) Throw it like a baseball; when you finish your throw, your arm should come down beside your leg. Throw your boomerang at a slight upward angle, almost straight ahead. Snap the boomerang out of your hand when you throw it, because if the boomerang doesn't spin, it doesn't return.

Don't expect it to come right back to your hand on the first throw! Practice the basics described here and you'll figure it out.

At some point, your boomerang will come right back to you. This is when you should panic! Scream *"Look out!"* and run away. This will provide anyone watching with a good laugh. After you're done messing around, try again. Keep your face out of its way! When the boomerang returns, catch it with two hands. If you don't know where it is, turn your back and clasp your hands on the back of your head. That way it won't break your face.

WHY DO YOU WEAR A HELMET WHEN YOU THROW YOUR BOOMERANG?

YOU'LL SEE!

Making Your Own Boomerangs

1. CLASSROOM SNEAKY SIZE: Okay, you're in class and you're sort of paying attention, but you need something to distract you. Get a 3 x 5-inch card, or any piece of paper made with card stock. Trace a boomerang

> *QUESTION:* What do you call a boomerang that doesn't work?
>
> *ANSWER:* A stick.

shape onto it; make it about 2 inches long. Next, cut it out. Slightly bend up the right-hand side tip. Gently hold the boomerang against a book, and tilt the book up a bit. Now flick it; it should come back! Experiment with different shapes!

2. *CLASSROOM NOT-SO-SNEAKY SIZE:* Try using any thin cardboard for this, like a manila folder or cardboard box. Just like above, trace a boomerang shape onto it, but make it 4 to 5 inches large. Bend each of the wings up somewhat: Hold it like a real boomerang (see earlier instructions), and throw by pinching it with your thumb and throwing it like a dart.

3. *PAINT STICK/RULER BOOMERANGS (OUTSIDE ONLY):* This is very easy. Take 2 paint-stirring sticks or rulers (wood or plastic), and use

Super Glue or rubber bands to stick them together at the halfway point to form an X. Bend each wing slightly up; don't break them! Throw like a regular boomerang. If it spins but doesn't return, try bending the wings more.

Paintball

Paintball is a very new game. It got its start in 1981, and although it requires a lot of specialized equipment, it has been very successful. Two big reasons for this success are that paintball is really fun and really intense! Of course, the key to winning at paintball is not to be hit *by* the paintball! These small balls are made of gelatin with a drop of colored liquid inside. Although they can be messy, paintballs are biodegradable, meaning they break down naturally.

A paintball gun is an air gun, just like BB guns. It uses compressed gas cartridges to fire the paintballs. These balls should never be moving more than 300 feet a second. At that speed, they will hurt (and even bruise) when they hit someone, but that's it. However, they could easily put out your eye, so players use headgear to protect themselves.

More than any other game, paintball is like war, though with a difference: there are referees to make sure nobody cheats! As you probably know, in paintball games, two teams literally fight it out. Paintballers often play a version of "capture the flag." Any player who gets shot is "dead" and must lie down or leave the field. Games can be as short as 10 minutes or they can go on for hours and hours.

I have played paintball before, and it is very exciting and exhausting! There is nothing as exhilarating as knocking an opponent out with a good shot, or as disappointing as getting shot yourself! I have learned that whatever version of paintball is played, the keys to victory are

Germ Warfare?

Modern countries have outlawed "germ warfare" (using diseases as a weapon), but it has been around for a long time, even before people knew what germs were. During the Middle Ages, dead and rotting animal carcasses were sometimes shot by catapult into towns under siege. The animal would land, explode, and release unhealthy germs into the surrounding air.

teamwork, skill, bravery, and luck. (Being sneaky and treacherous can also help.)

Slingshots

A slingshot can be a handheld weapon or something much bigger. Maybe you've seen a catapult before; a catapult is just a big slingshot that can

265

throw giant rocks! (For detailed plans on how to make an impressive catapult, see the book *Backyard Ballistics* by William Gurstelle.)

If you want a store-bought slingshot or wrist rocket, go buy one. It is also very easy to make your own mini-slingshot out of a big paperclip and a rubber band, but I'll assume that you can do that.

But back in the *old* days, when a boy used a sling, it was just as deadly as a wrist rocket, and it required a bit of skill. That *sling* was a long strap of leather (usually) with a pouch in the middle. One end of the sling had a loop for your finger, and the other end was straight.

The idea of using it is simple. Wrap the loop around your finger. Put a rock or marble in the pouch. Take the other end of the sling and clench it between your thumb and forefinger. Twirl it over your head. Aim at an object and let go of the end of the sling! At first, the rock you throw may end up just about anywhere, so practice this in a park. After you improve, you may get quite accurate. Maybe you could clock that Goliath kid who's been bothering you!

★ *DO NOT GET IN A ROCK FIGHT WITH THESE GUYS!* An ancient Spanish tribe called the Baleares used slings that threw stones weighing over a pound. The velocity of the rocks could smash through armor.

★**MORE FUN WITH ROCKS!** Everyone knows that if you have a smooth oval stone, some flat water, and a good sideways throw, you can do some serious rock skipping. What you may not know is that you can also skip stones on sand. If you're at the beach, go to the wet sand. Throw a stone at the sand as if it were water. It won't skip as far as it would on water, but it'll skip!

Water Balloons

Water balloons are the weapon of choice for most boys. They combine the risk of a hand grenade with the joy of getting someone wet!

Whether you're in a water balloon duel or a water balloon toss, here are some basic tips:

FILLING THE BALLOON: You don't want to fill the balloon too much if you can help it. More water equals more pressure . . . which equals you being wet!

THROWING THE BALLOON: If you are in a water balloon toss, then you want to make a nice, smooth, underhand throw with a high arc. Your hand should start way behind you and end up over your head after your release!

If you are in a water balloon war, all bets are off! You don't have time to think about how you throw it, but if you do, remember not to make any sudden throwing movements, or it will just burst on you!

CATCHING THE BALLOON: The key to making a successful catch is not to offer the balloon any resistance. Meet the balloon with both of your hands in front of you, and then let your hands travel with the balloon; don't try to stop it, just slow it down. Go with it! This is how to win the balloon toss, and how to turn the tables on your opponent in the water balloon war! Nothing is more impressive than catching your opponent's balloon, whipping it around, and throwing it back at him.

ESCAPING THE BALLOON: Three words—duck and dodge! If your opponent is faster than you, run away as fast as you can. When you can hear your opponent's footsteps getting near, drop to the ground! He may just miss you with the balloon, or he might trip over you and fall on his own balloon!

Bonus Water Balloon Information

FUN WATER BALLOON TRICK: You know how a magnifying glass can focus the sun's rays into a hot point? Well, balloons can only stand this kind of heat for an *instant* before they blow. Think of creative ways you can use this laser device to create mischief.

GENERAL STRATEGY: In any war, you want the high ground. It is easier to defend yourself and harder for someone else to attack you. If you are higher than your water balloon opponent (say, on a hill or picnic bench), you can see where they are and you have gravity on your side when you throw down on them.

Water Balloon Duel

One of the best games to play with water balloons is Water Balloon Duel. You and your friend each get a filled balloon and stand back-to-back. Then you loudly count to three; with each number called, you both take a step. After you get to three, you both turn and duel! You can throw your balloon, or run away, or run toward your opponent and try to get him right in the face . . . but once your balloon is gone, go into evasive maneuvers!

Follow~Up Activity

Throughout history, there have been a number of ballistae that shot "arrows" that were bigger than spears! Make your own ballista and use it for target practice!

FOR A LIST of this book's sources, visit http://www.bartking.net

ACKNOWLEDGMENTS ·

People who were helpful in contributing to this book in one misguided way or another include Dallas Wassink, Matt & Melinda Grow, Troy Taylor, Peter Ford, Mary Groh, the Judds, Erik King, Simon Wintle, Richard Feely, Linda Holt, the Twomeys, Kristin Heintz, Kris, Oliver and Michael King, Kelby Smith, Tanner Johnson, Dan Ryan, Mary Falkenstein, Jenny Ball, Andrew Simon, Michael Lepene, Kay Moore, Marcus Triest, Jim Murai, Sean Fronczak, Peter King, Mary Wiley, Anita Phillips, Genevieve Smith, and Brody vanderSommen. Many thanks!

Finally, to my wife Lynn: Much love and thanks for your help and support.